SEXUAL IDENTITY SYNTHESIS

*Attributions, Meaning-Making,
and the Search for Congruence*

Mark A. Yarhouse

Erica S. N. Tan

University Press of America,® Inc.
Lanham · Boulder · New York · Toronto · Oxford

Copyright © 2004 by
University Press of America,® Inc.
4501 Forbes Boulevard
Suite 200
Lanham, Maryland 20706
UPA Acquisitions Department (301) 459-3366

PO Box 317
Oxford
OX2 9RU, UK

Library of Congress Control Number: 2004111487
ISBN 0-7618-2984-9 (paperback : alk. ppr.)

The little that we know would continue to be unknown if it were not for those who freely and courageously shared their experiences with us. Nor would we have had the opportunity to record these experiences were it not for the community gatekeepers who gave us access. Thank you. This work is dedicated to you.

—Mark & Erica

Contents

Acknowledgments

For the past several years our research team at Regent University has been exploring and examining a number of issues related to sexual identity. Our focus has been on how to best understand and convey what happens when people of faith experience same-sex attraction. How do they sort out the complexities of the intersection that brings together religion, spirituality, sexual attraction, and behavior?

Religious communities in general, and the Christian church in particular, have to think more deeply about these issues. Emerging developments in sexual identity theory may provide clues as to how to articulate a theology of human sexuality while making practical, pastoral application that affects the lives of those who experience same-sex attraction. To make progress in the debates in the church and in the broader culture, we need to move, we believe, in the direction of identity. What does it mean to develop a sexual identity? What factors influence such an identity? How does a religious identity inform a person's sexual identity and vice versa?

Our interest in sexual identity, homosexuality, and the religious and spiritual issues facing those who experience same-sex attraction began several years ago. For Mark these interests were tied to the instruction and mentoring received through his work with Stanton Jones, Provost and Professor of Psychology at Wheaton College. Their work together led to a co-authored resource titled, *Homosexuality: The Use of Scientific Research in the Church's Moral Debate*. Interest continued through Mark's clinical practice and research on sexual identity at Regent University, where William Hathaway and several faculty members in the School of Psychology and Counseling have served as catalysts for reflection from a Christian worldview. The most recent development is the establishment of the Institute for the Study of Sexual Identity, which provides a forum for ongoing research, training, and clinical intervention/consulta-

tion. For Erica these interests were elicited by two different, yet comple-
mentary avenues simultaneously: academia and ministry. As a new member of Mark's research team at Regent University, she was exposed to
research and theories about sexual identity development that articulated
at a clinical level the experiences of individuals with whom she had contact in a local para-church ministry. These concordant experiences fu-
eled a desire to better understand the communities that seek to integrate
their faith with their sexual identities. Consequently, two research studies cited in this book were developed as attempts to uncover the stories of
individuals in these communities.

We are especially grateful to the individuals within both the Universal Fellowship of Metropolitan Community Churches and the Exodus-
affiliated ministries who served as gatekeepers to their respective communities, and to those individuals who were willing to trust us with their
experiences. Research and writing on sexual identity has also led to numerous e-mail exchanges and opportunities to present papers and consult
in a variety of settings; these exchanges are always helpful and edifying
in one way or another. Regent University and the Faculty Senate have
supported us with research grants to work on the Sexual Identity Project,
for which we are deeply grateful. We are also thankful to the students at
the Institute for the Study of Sexual Identity, several of whom tracked
down articles, commented on rough drafts, and engaged us in discussions on these issues. We want to especially recognize Stephen Russell,
Heather Brooke, Robyn Seymore, and Edye Garcia for the contributions
they have made.

We are particularly grateful to outside readers, including A. Lee
Beckstead, Ariel Shidlo, Lori Burkett, Gary Strauss, and several anonymous reviewers for their comments on our manuscript. As always, we
have benefited from their insights and critiques, but we are responsible
for the final manuscript, warts and all. Mark would also like to thank his
wife, Lori, and their children, Lynnea, Peter, and Celia, for their love,
support, and encouragement. Erica would like to thank her parents, Kok-
Swang and Ruth, her brother, Chris, and many friends who have encouraged her to pursue and enjoy challenges throughout her studies. She
would also like to thank Mark for his mentorship and the opportunities
he has provided to help her become a steward of what she has learned.

Part 1

Foundations

Chapter 1

Models of Sexual Identity Development

Introduction

Sexual identity is a broad construct that has emerged as an increasingly important concept in the study of human sexuality and sexual behavior. *Sexual identity* refers to one's self-designation according to one's sense of biological sex, gender, orientation, behavior, and values; it is influenced by both Nature and Nurture and is a complex and multifaceted construct.

To unpack the construct further, a person's biological sex is either male or female. Biological sex contributes to one's overall sexual identity, as does the sense of being either masculine or feminine (gender identity). Orientation, while often a focal point in debates about same-sex attraction and behavior, refers to the direction of one's sexual attractions toward the same, or opposite sex, or both. Behavior, too, is an important aspect of sexual identity. We refer here to what a person does with the attractions he or she has. Behavior, in this context, can help consolidate a sexual identity, as specific acts may be both an expression of and a bridge toward one's sense of self as a sexual being. The last major area relative to sexual identity is what we think of as a valuative framework, or one's beliefs and values about the ethics of particular behavior. One aspect of being human is that we reflect upon our actions and often look to sources outside ourselves and our inclinations to help us evaluate the morality and ethics of our behavior. These evaluations also contribute to a person's sense of sexual identity.

Vivian Cass, an important early theorist on sexual identity development and synthesis, discussed homosexual identity, or one's sense of self as homosexual. She noted that "Homosexual identity . . . evolves out of a clustering of self-images which are linked together by the individual's idiosyncratic understanding of what characterizes someone as 'a homosexual.'"[1] This includes the perceptions of oneself as homosexual in the eyes of others who are significant to that individual. According to Cass, *sexual orientation* refers to one's physical and sexual attractions—including an interest in developing a romantic or emotionally engaging relationship—for members of the same, or opposite-sex, or both. Thus, as has been suggested, sexual orientation is a substructure, which is subsumed under the construct of sexual identity.

Before we further examine the construct of sexual identity, it is important to mention the metaphysical debate on the definition of sexual orientation, as well as theories about the etiology of sexual orientation. A vigorous debate is underway about what sexual orientation actually *is*. The debate is typically characterized as being between essentialists and constructionists. From the essentialist position, sexual orientation is regarded as a real thing (as with the distinction of biological sex made between male and female). The categories of heterosexual, homosexual, and bisexual are thought to be "natural human kinds"[2] that are important core components of the self as a person. Essentialists are typically united in their claim that sexual orientation is an enduring reality, stable across cultures and time; some essentialists go further:

> The first and most explicit claim is that homosexuality, or sexual orientation more generally, is an enduring and universal reality, an essence. . . . Second, some (but not all) essentialists argue that this essence is ineluctably bound to the core of one's self as a particular human being. The third claim often follows from the second: because this real essence is a part of what properly defines the core for the person, homosexual behavior is naturally occurring, morally blameless behavior that should find expression.[3]

Many essentialists—though not all—turn to research suggesting that biology plays a role in the etiology of sexual orientation.

On the other side of the debate is the viewpoint that sexual orientation is socially constructed, that is, an individual's sense of sexual preference is shaped by the social or historical context in which one grows up. Sexual orientation, rather than being a "real" thing, is thought to be a linguistic construct fashioned by society to describe sexual preferences. In this sense, to identify as gay is similar to identifying as a Republican or a Democrat. These labels are "social human kinds"[4] and are meaningful only in our culture at this point in history. The labels themselves can provide some information about a person's political preferences, but they are neither stable nor are they universal constructs recognized through history and across cultures.

By only considering the "broad-brush" nature of these two perspectives, and not accounting for underlying factors (e.g., biology, environmental factors) that support these two metaphysical viewpoints, researchers and others risk oversimplifying the process by which individuals decide that they are (or are not) lesbian, gay, or bisexual (LGB). However, most scholars today agree that both Nature and Nurture contribute to what we call sexual orientation, regardless of whether one endorses essentialism or constructionism.

One recently proposed hypothesis for the etiology of a homosexual orientation is referred to as the "weighted interactionist hypothesis."[5] According to this perspective, the interaction of four broad clusters of factors formulate one's experience of persistent same-sex attraction. The concentration and composition of these factors differs (or is "weighted" differently) from person to person. The factors are (1) *biological antecedents*, (2) *childhood experiences*, (3) *environmental influences*, and (4) *adult experiences* (e.g., one's volitional pursuit of same-sex behavior).

Evidence to support any one of these four weighted factors is equivocal. For example, although there was a significant push during the 1990s to suggest that biological antecedents caused homosexuality, the research is rather mixed, with several initially suggestive studies failing replication. In a number of the most promising studies, for example, those comparing identical and fraternal twins of homosexuals, researchers found that evidence pointing to a significant genetic contribution is not nearly as robust as was originally thought.[6] Similarly, research on a chromosomal marker initially suggested a genetic marker for a specific subtype of homosexuality,[7] but follow-up research has not confirmed this, and in one case, the researchers could not find the marker at all.[8] Moreover, research supporting the prenatal hormonal hypothesis—that prenatal hormones contribute to the later development of a homosexual orientation— is mixed. Some of the most widely-publicized findings[9] have been the most susceptible to methodological critique, and other findings,[10] while initially suggestive, seem to correspond to regions of neuroanatomical brain structures that have no known influence on human sexual behavior. Nevertheless, it is certainly possible that various biological antecedents provide a "push" in the direction of homosexuality for some individuals (that is, biology may be weighted in the direction of homosexuality for certain persons), and that the push might represent temperamental and personality idiosyncracies.

Research on childhood experiences is also equivocal. Research on parent-child relationships has been mixed, with some studies supporting the classic detached/critical father and over-involved mother,[11] while other studies apparently do not support the theory or else they support a variation on the theory for some individuals.[12] The studies are not of the highest validity, though they were of comparable methodological sophistication as other studies conducted at that time. With further regard to the influence of childhood experiences on sexual identity, research suggests that early sexual abuse is reported by a higher percentage of adults who identify as LGB (as compared to adults who do not self-identify as LGB).[13] However, greater numbers of people who have experienced sexual abuse do not later self-identify as LGB, and not all persons who identify as LGB have experienced sexual abuse.

Environmental factors, such as sociocultural messages that facilitate sexual disinhibition and experimentation may also play a role in same-sex behavior, which may further consolidate a sexual orientation. For example, Gagnon[14] reviews research showing that prevalence rates among men who identify as homosexual rose from 1.3% (rural) to 9.2% (urban) (with a 2.8% general prevalence rate in the general population).[15] These findings held true for women who identified as lesbians: 2.6% (urban) versus 1.4% (general) and < 1% rural. The obvious question is whether these elevations are due to migration, and that may be the case; but the differences are also noted in adolescents aged 14-16. In this way both environmental factors and volition (as suggested by intentional experimentation) may play a role in sexual orientation.

The focus of this book is neither on sexual orientation nor the persistence and directionality of one's erotic attractions. Rather, our emphasis is to analyze how these factors and many others come to shape an individual's experience of sexual identity (of which sexual orientation is but one dimension). This book then is about the perceived milestone experiences of those who pass through what is referred to as sexual identity development and achieve a kind of synthesis or consolidation of their sexual identity. Before we turn to a review of several theories of sexual identity development and synthesis, we would like to discuss additional factors, such as attractions and behaviors, which may shape one's sexual identity.

Same-Sex Attraction, Behavior, and Identification

In their comprehensive study of sexual practices in the United States, Laumann and his colleagues examined three dimensions of homosexuality they believed would help elucidate the varying prevalence rates: same-sex behavior, same-sex desire, and self-identification as gay or lesbian. In their study, same-sex desire and identity were understood to echo the participants' "current state[s] of mind."[16] The researchers evaluated same-sex sexual behavior at three different time periods in the lives of their respondents: the past year (12 months), the past five years, and since turning 18 years old. The rates of same-sex behavior for women varied between 1.3% of women reporting same-sex sexual behavior in the last year and 4.1% of women who experienced same-sex behavior since age 18. For these same periods of time, the percentages reported for men were 2.7% and 4.9%, respectively.[17] Of the individuals who revealed engaging in sexual behavior at any age since puberty, 3.8% of women and 7.1% of men acknowledged this practice.[18] Similar figures were reported for women and men who experienced any sexual behavior with a member of the same sex—over 4% of women and 9% of men reported such sexual activity. A comparable percentage of men and women (about 5% for each, respectively) reported experiencing same-sex sexual attraction and regarded same-sex behavior as appealing.[19] In this study, percentages reported for same-sex sexual behaviors, as opposed to actual self-identification as homosexual, were higher: 1.4% of women and 2.8% of men identified as homosexual.[20] In analyzing the results of their study, Laumann et al. confirm:

> . . . the high degree of variability in the way that different elements of homosexuality are distributed in the population. This variability relates to the way that homosexuality is both organized as a set of behaviors and practices and experienced subjectively. It raises quite provocative questions about the definition of *homosexuality*.[21]

Consequently, Laumann et al. emphasized that ". . . no single number can be used to provide an accurate and valid characterization of the incidence and prevalence of homosexuality in the population at large."[22]

What is particularly interesting about Laumann et al.'s findings regarding the prevalence rates of homosexuality is that participation in same-sex behavior did not consistently translate into self-identification as homosexual. It is certainly plausible that internal factors (e.g., emotional attractions, personal values), external factors (e.g., peer and familial relationships, societal expectations), as well as the interaction of these and a host of other factors, contribute to one's sexual identity development and synthesis.

From a clinical perspective, these influences cannot be underestimated by therapists who work with clients who experience same-sex attraction and are not yet certain of their sexual identification. "The therapist's primary task with such individuals is to suspend all assumptions and to lead an exploration with often difficult questions," such as, "If [you] were to self-identify as homosexual, what losses would [you] potentially face?" or "How would [you] cope with [your anxieties] as a homosexual individual?"[23] By the same token, Haldeman exhorts therapists to assist but not direct clients in "how to live their lives". He urges that they be keenly aware of the potential pitfalls of personal bias in facilitating the process of helping clients explore the meaning of experiences of same-sex attraction. Clients who have these feelings and experiences need the safety of a therapist whose own personal beliefs (e.g., gay-affirming or non-affirming) do not become an agenda:

> Erotic identities, because of the erotonegativism of our culture, are especially likely to have changing rather than fixed values and meanings. Identifications are just landmarks of the process Erickson calls ego identity. The central function of this process is to integrate various identifications into a healthy sense of self: a self with a pleasurable and conscious sense of continuity and community. . . . The therapeutic goal is to create an environment that allows patients to explore safely their particular array of erotic identifications and determine for themselves how best to synthesize or abandon them.[24]

Thus, the development of sexual identification as gay, lesbian, bisexual, or heterosexual tends to be a complex process that involves myriad influences.[25] Sexual identification is not merely the recognition of sexual feelings directed towards either members of the same—or opposite—sex.

Instead, it includes the integration of personal internal and external experiences, which may validate or deny one's feelings of sexual attraction. Several models of sexual identity formation have been formulated, which suggest that a number of factors indeed influence this process of self-identification. We will therefore focus in this chapter on several models of general homosexual identity development, gay male identity development, and lesbian sexual identity development.[26] We address heterosexual identity development, bisexual and ethnic minority sexual identity considerations, and additional emerging trends in sexual identity development theory in Chapter 2.

General Models of Homosexual Identity Development

Models of general homosexual identity formation vary in their approach to conceptualization of this process. Some models consider the influence of social factors on sexual identity development, albeit from different perspectives. Thus, a wide array of perspectives is presented in terms of understanding how homosexual identity development might take place at a general level (see Table 1).

The Cass Model

One of the most commonly cited theories of general homosexual identity development is Cass' model,[27] which bears two assumptions: identity is a developmental process and identification depends on the interaction between individuals and their environment. Within the six stages of identity development proposed, *identity foreclosure* (i.e., merely assuming a heterosexual identification without any further exploration, thus resulting in the rejection of a homosexual identity) is possible at each stage. The process of achieving a homosexual identity depends on the ability to attain congruency between oneself, one's behavior, and one's perception of other people as gay or lesbian, which either receives support or disapproval, depending on one's social environment. Cass acknowledges that, prior to giving personal meaning to homosexuality, a person's self image is heterosexual.

The first stage is *identity confusion*, whereby thoughts, feelings, and behaviors perceived as homosexual are experienced as incongruent with

Sexual Identity Synthesis

Table 1. *Theories of General Sexual Identity Development*

	Cass (1979)	Coleman (1982)	Troiden (1989)	Grace (1992)
Stage 1	Identity confusion	Pre-coming out: preconscious awareness	Sensitization	Emergence
Stage 2	Identity comparison	Coming out: Self-admission	Identity confusion	Acknowledgment
Stage 3	Identity tolerance	Exploration: Testing, contact with the gay community	Identity assumption	Find community
Stage 4	Identity acceptance	First relationship	Commitment	First relationships (from dream world to disillusionment to enlightenment to mutual respect)
Stage 5	Identity pride	Integration		Self-definition and reintegration
Stage 6	Identity synthesis			

Note: The models of general sexual identity development proposed by Cox and Gallois and Horowitz and Newcomb are not represented because they are not stage models as such.

the individual's former conception of a fairly consistent and stable situation. In this instance, the individual experiences "affective confusion" and tries to figure out, "Who am I?" Cass[28] identifies three possible solutions to confused feelings at this stage: (1) the individual accepts that the meaning of the behavior is correct, (2) the individual forecloses his or her sexual identity because the meaning of the behavior is unwanted, even though it may be correct, and (3) the individual forecloses his or her sexual identity because the meaning of the behavior is unwanted and incorrect.

Identity comparison is the second stage. In this stage, the individual considers that perhaps a homosexual identity is possible. The developmental task at this point is for the individual to work through any experiences of social alienation while handling feelings of incongruency due to a past identification as heterosexual. Meanwhile, the individual attempts to reconfigure guidelines of behavior, ideals, and expectations meant for a heterosexual identity. Cass (1991) outlines four approaches to the identity comparison stage: (1) the individual experiences a positive reaction to the idea of being different, (2) the meaning of the behavior is acceptable, but unwanted, thus leading the individual to adopt a stance as "a special case," as "ambisexual," "as merely a temporary identity," or that one bears no "responsibility" for the experience, (3) although the behaviors and the individual's self-conception has "homosexual meaning," the behavior is undesirable; hence, one experiences inhibition leading to an asexual role or asexual self-image, which in essence, is considered identity foreclosure, and (4) identity foreclosure occurs because an individual rejects both homosexual self identity and behavior.

During the *identity tolerance* stage, one considers the possibility of being homosexual and starts to acknowledge social, emotional, and sexual needs. Relationships with other homosexuals begin to increase while there occurs a simultaneous detachment from heterosexuals. Interaction with other homosexuals now becomes crucial, because unrewarding contacts with the gay subculture lead to the devaluation of the individual's homosexual identity and experience. At this stage, Cass avers that successful inhibition of same-sex behaviors leads to identity foreclosure.

The fourth stage, *identity acceptance*, is characterized by increased levels of contact with other homosexuals (or what would today be referred to as the "gay community") as well as one's acceptance of a homosexual self-image. The individual is becoming aware of the importance of a gay subculture and is trying to reduce incongruent feelings by selectively disclosing a homosexual sexual identity to significant heterosexuals.

In the *identity pride* stage, the individual has moved beyond mere self-acceptance as homosexual and become increasingly aware of the discrepancy between self-approval and societal rejection of homosexuality. In retaliation, one may start to devalue heterosexuality and cope by dichotomizing the society into homosexual versus heterosexual. By being strongly committed to the gay culture, the individual becomes less concerned with heterosexual opinion, and experiences congruence between his or her public and private self as homosexual.

The final stage in Cass's model is *identity synthesis*, during which time the individual's homosexual identity is integrated into other aspects of the self. In addition, because one's sexual identity is no longer regarded as a defining feature, one no longer assumes that all heterosexuals are negative and all homosexuals are positive.

The Coleman Model

In contrast to Cass's linear model of sexual identity development, Coleman's[29] five-stage model presumes the simultaneous pursuit of several developmental tasks. Other assumptions of his model include the recognition that not everyone will proceed through all five stages, and that sexual identity integration (i.e., identifying as lesbian, gay, or bisexual) may not be experienced by some. The first stage is *pre-coming out*, which refers to the occurrence in childhood where both the individual and the family members sense that he or she is "different"; this may exacerbate or be exacerbated by low self-esteem. Consequently, these individuals might attempt to protect themselves from an awareness of their difference—which equates with vulnerability—by developing defenses (e.g., repression, rationalization, etc.). As Coleman puts it, "Because individuals at the pre-coming out stage are not consciously aware of their same-sex feelings, they cannot describe what is wrong."[30] One developmental task is to work through feeling different (i.e., the "existential crisis")[31] by considering the experience of same-sex attraction as possibly being legitimate (in which legitimacy is linked with who a person "really is").

The first developmental task of the *coming out* stage is the acknowledgement of feelings of same-sex attraction; however, some individuals might not accept that this might be a precursor to a homosexual identity. According to Coleman, awareness of same-sex attraction develops between the ages of 13 and 18 years. After individuals have recognized their feelings of same-sex attraction, the next developmental task is to disclose this information to others. The purpose of this undertaking is to initiate self-acceptance, because "the perceived status of the person disclosed to greatly affects the possibility of self-concept change in the individual."[32]

An individual enters the *exploration* stage when one begins to test his or her "new" identity by interacting with others who also experience same-sex attraction. As Coleman indicates, "The opportunity to interact with others who are open and honest about their sexuality furthers the development of a positive self-image."[33] In this stage, the first developmental task·is to cultivate interpersonal skills in order to facilitate interaction with others who experience same-sex attraction. The second task is to develop a sense of competency in the area of sexuality, in conjunction with a "sense of personal attractiveness."[34] This development of sexual competence is followed by an increased understanding that sexual preference is not the only component of identity. Coleman specifies the use of self-medication (e.g., drug abuse, alcoholism, and promiscuity) as deterrents against the angst and pain of identity exploration; however, these activities can potentially hinder the completion of developmental tasks during this stage.

After a period of sexual exploration devoid of intimacy, an individual realizes the need and desire for a deeper connection with another person, at which point he or she enters into a *first relationship*. In this fourth stage, the developmental task entails learning how to operate in a same-sex relationship that is circumscribed by a heterosexual society. However, Coleman notes that first relationships tend to disintegrate due to the incomplete integration of the homosexual identity with one's constituent parts. This can manifest as a negative perception of homosexuality, or a lack of trust and possessiveness within the relationship.

The final stage of Coleman's model is the *integration* stage, which is characterized by the consolidation of the private and public identities into one self-image. Individuals at this stage of sexual identity development tend to be more successful in intimate relationships because they are more flexible and forgiving. Concurrently, terminations of relationships are not as injurious to an individual's self-concept.

The Troiden Model

Troiden's[35] model of what was then referred to as general homosexual identity development is based on sociological theory (i.e., sexuality is defined by society). According to his model, sexual feelings are identified and labeled according to socially constructed gender roles and sexual scripts. However, before an individual can begin to identify within a particular social category, one needs to learn (1) that feelings are reflected in a social category, (2) that others also have membership in that category, (3) that members of that social category share more similarities than differences, (4) how to identify with others in that social category, (5) how to qualify for membership in that category, (6) to label oneself in terms of the social category, and (7) to incorporate these identities into a self-concept.

As with Coleman's pre-coming out stage, Troiden's first stage—*sensitization*—occurs before puberty whereby an assumption is held that the individual is heterosexual. However, this individual experiences feelings of marginality, of difference from other same-sex peers. At this time, sexual experimentation is not defined according to "heterosexual" or "homosexual" labels, and is significant to the process of sensitization, because meaning is attributed to childhood experience. Experiences of sexual experimentation are later reinterpreted through memory recall as a homosexual propensity, which eventually facilitates the adoption of a homosexual sexual identity.

Troiden's second stage—*identity confusion*—is conceptually similar to that of Cass. During adolescence, homosexuality becomes personalized. The adolescent experiences inner turmoil and uncertainty about an ambiguous sexual status. Identity confusion may be caused by several different factors: altered perceptions of the self, experiences of both homosexual and heterosexual arousal and behavior, the stigma surrounding homosexuality, and inaccurate knowledge about homosexuals and homosexuality.Individuals in this stage might, as a consequence, attempt to respond to the identity confusion with: (1) *denial* of the feelings and the identity, (2) *repair* attempts (e.g., efforts to eradicate homosexual feelings), (3) *avoidance* (e.g., inhibit behaviors, restrict exposure only to the opposite sex, avoid information about homosexuality, assume an anti-homosexual view, heterosexual immersion, or escapism), (4) *redefinition* (e.g., "I am an isolated case," "I am ambisexual," "This is a temporary identity," or explain the experience as "situation versus self"), or (5) *acceptance* that this is who one "really is."

During the *identity assumption* stage of Troiden's model, individuals who experience same-sex attraction assume a homosexual identity that characterizes their self-image and their presentation to others. There are, however, distinctions between the experiences of lesbians and gay males. For example, whereas lesbians tend to acquire homosexual self-identification within the context of intense affectionate relationships with other women, gay males acquire a homosexual self-definition within "sociosexual" contexts; these positive contacts with other gay or lesbian individuals facilitate homosexual identification because it provides a basis for re-examination and re-evaluation of ideas concerning homosexuality. Behaviors of individuals in this stage vary widely between "minstrelization"—behaving in a highly stereotyped manner—and passing as a heterosexual. The individual may at some point experience group alignment, which confirms membership of that individual into the world of homosexuals. An individual who participates in undesirable homosexual experiences may reject the identity, abandon the behavior, or both.

The last stage of Troiden's model is the *commitment* stage, which is characterized by the adoption of homosexuality as a way of life both internally and externally. Several processes occur internally: (1) sexuality and emotionality fuse, thus indicating a commitment to a gay-affirming ideology, (2) the meaning attached to a homosexual identity changes, (3) the individual feels that a homosexual identity is a valid self-identity, (4) the individual experiences satisfaction with a homosexual identity, and (5) the individual feels greater happiness after defining herself or himself as lesbian or gay.

Changes in the individual's commitment to a gay-affirming ideology also occur externally. The person (1) engages in same-sex love relationships, (2) discloses a homosexual identity to heterosexuals, and (3) and makes changes in his or her stigma-management strategies (i.e., strategies include "covering"—admitting his or her homosexuality, but preventing it from looming large, "blending"—displays gender-appropriate behaviors, but neither announces nor denies one's homosexuality, and "converting"—confronting the homosexual stigma). Once an individual reaches the *commitment* stage, sexual identity development does not cease; the person's commitment to a homosexual identity constantly evolves and is somewhat variable, in that it is influenced by various social, personal, and professional factors.

The Grace Model

Grace's model[36] of sexual identity formation differs from previous models by its clarification of homophobia as an impediment to the sexual identity process. In particular, this five-stage model considers both active and passive expressions of homophobia within personal and institutional relationships.

The first stage of Grace's model, *emergence*, is similar to Troiden's *sensitization* and Coleman's *pre-coming out* stages, which describe the experience that some individuals felt different from their peers as children. This feeling of difference is not naturally attributed to same-sex attraction at this stage; however, it is sufficient to cause feelings of shame, which induce performance and social anxiety. From within this model, the shame associated with feeling different might be thought of as a precursor to homophobia, but certainly not at the conscious level.

Acknowledgement is Grace's second stage, which is likened to the Troiden and Cass stage of *identity confusion*.[37] Individuals in this stage are aware of their same-sex attractions as a result of experiences such as homoerotic fantasies; however, they still feel deep shame and fear about these feelings and will tend to continue "passing" as heterosexuals. Again, from this model, this internalized homophobia evokes further feelings of anxiety, because the person is aware of posturing without authenticity. At this stage, some individuals might foreclose on a gay or lesbian identity because of internalized homophobia.

The personal acknowledgement of a gay or lesbian identity is usually followed by public recognition. As such, many individuals try to *find community* where they can share their private identities as lesbian or gay with others who understand. This time is also referred to as the emotional developmental stage of "gay and lesbian adolescence," whereby individuals seek to make up for their perceived time lost as "pseudo-heterosexuals." Similar to the actual developmental stage of adolescence, this emotional adolescence tends to be characterized by emotional tumult, which may cause some individuals to foreclose on a gay or lesbian identity.

A lesbian or gay identity is further solidified by engagement in *first relationships*. According to Ritter and Terndrup, these first relationships tend to follow a common progression: dream world stage (idealizing the other partner), disillusionment stage (more realistic perception develops), misery (potential termination of the relationship due to internalized shame), enlightenment (responsibility for successful relationship assumed), and mutual respect (commitment to the relationship through consideration of strengths, weaknesses, similarities, and differences).

The last stage of Grace's model is *self-definition and reintegration*, which is portrayed as a developmental stage that traverses one's lifetime as the individual learns and re-configures the meaning of human identity.

The Cox and Gallois Model

Several models cited[38] identify external factors as influences of sexual identity formation. The Cox and Gallois model,[39] based on social identity theory, examines the impact of social forces on the developmental process of identity acquisition, and how the process of identity development affects social structures. Although this is not a "stage model" like the other conceptualizations, it is useful in its consideration of sexual identity development as a process-oriented phenomenon.

According to social identity theory, there are two processes: (1) *self-categorization*, which results in the development of several social identities, and (2) *social comparison*, which is directed towards ameliorating self-esteem. Thus, "Self-categorization is not merely an act of self-labeling, but an adoption over time of the normative (prototypical) behaviors, characteristics, and values associated with the particular group membership."[40]

Individuals have a social identity and a personal identity, and an individual's self-concept comprises these two aspects. According to Cox and Gallois, social identity consists of the particular aspects of oneself, which contribute to group membership and are shared with individuals who also possess those same aspects. An individual therefore has many social identities, which may contribute to either increased or decreased self-esteem, depending on whether the person possesses many "minority" identities, how they feel about those identities, and what support they receive for their various identities. For example, Cox and Gallois posit that individuals with multiple "minority" identities (e.g., an Asian lesbian) might have a greater difficulty developing a healthy self-esteem because of the additive effects of the negative reactions they possibly encounter regarding minority group memberships. All the behaviors, values, and traits that distinguish one individual from another are conceptualized as the personal identity.

The process of social comparison enables individuals to develop social and personal identities by choosing components of their group or individual distinctions to compare with other groups or individuals. If the comparisons result in these individuals feeling better about themselves, then their self-esteem is heightened. This in turn strengthens that particular aspect of their identity (social or personal). Thus, the similarity in processes for acquiring social and personal identities also lends to the possibility that what one individual considers to be essential to personal identity might also be regarded as essential to another person's social identity.

Therefore, according to Cox and Gallois, two processes occur in the development of a homosexual identity. The first is self-categorization as homosexual, which gradually integrates into a personal identity, a social identity, or both. The second process of evaluation brings one to the realization that: "Once a person socially self-categorizes as homosexual, he or she is motivated to perceive the homosexual in-group in a positive light."[41]

The Horowitz and Newcomb Model

Horowitz and Newcomb[42] presented a multidimensional approach to considering general homosexual identity based on Cox and Gallois's gay and lesbian social identity development perspective, which they use as a framework to understand the experience and evaluation of desires, behavior, and identity as separate contributors to sexual identity. Employing a social constructionist position, Horowitz and Newcomb posit an inclusive model of sexual identity development in their attempt to portray the various trajectories: heterosexual, homosexual, bisexual, as well as other experiences inadequately described by the three labels. From this perspective, Horowitz and Newcomb aver ". . . the optimal or universal goal to be achieved is that the individual experiences sexuality in a positive light and has tolerance for diversity and ambiguity within oneself."[43]

According to this model, an individual's sexual identity develops as a result of social interactions in particular historical and social contexts. Along this vein, Horowitz and Newcomb posit that there might be some psychological distress experienced by those for whom sexuality may be somewhat ill fitting with respect to prescribed social categories. Specifically, the utility of social constructionist theory in explaining how sexual identity develops within society begins with the emphasis that "homosexual behavior and etiological factors"[44] have particular meaning for each person in their contribution to significant events in an individual's life experience. Thus, an individual's sexual identity develops as one begins to assimilate societal views of these factors, their interaction, and personal experience of these influences. As such, a cyclical pattern emerges: "The individual meanings we give to the factors will influence how we interact with the world and our life experiences which, in turn, affect the meanings we give to the factors."[45]

Horowitz and Newcomb propose that the strength of this model is the assertion that humans have a "more active role in the development of a healthy sexual identity"[46] as they seek to impart meaning onto the life experiences that promote sexual identity development and expression. Thus, "From the social constructionist perspective, what is important is the meaning the individual ascribes to the sexual desires, behaviors, and identity."[47]

As theorists reflected further on sexual identity development and synthesis, they began to realize that not everyone who identifies as homosexual has similar key milestone events. In fact, one of the first major distinctions understood by researchers was between males and females; that is, experiences differ between gay males and lesbians.[48]

Models of Gay Male Identity Development

Although sexual identity development for gays and lesbians may appear to follow similar trajectories, there are significant differences in the presentation of same-sex behaviors and the meanings of relationships. Although several theorists discuss sexual identity development within a general homosexual (or "gay") framework, increased attention has been given to distinct gay male and lesbian experience. A few models of gay male identity development are delineated here (see Table 2).

The McDonald Model

McDonald[49] reported on his study of 199 self-identified gay males and their recollection of milestone experiences along the path toward positive gay identification. McDonald found a sequential and temporal progression in the acquisition of a homosexual identity. In his sample, the average age of awareness of same-sex attraction was 13 years. The majority of respondents came to understand the meaning of the term "homosexual" two years later (age 15 years) and labeled themselves as homosexual at approximately age 19. On average, by the age of 21, the majority of participants had experienced their first relationship, and two years later, disclosed their homosexual identity to a heterosexual. Thus, in this sample, participants experienced homosexual behaviors between 13 to 15 years of age, and self-identification as homosexual occurred between ages 19 and 21. McDonald reported that participants who indicated that they lacked a positive gay identity, expressed negative attitudes about homosexuality, were not as involved in the gay subculture, did not disclose their sexuality as frequently to others, and experienced guilt and shame about their sexual preference. Conversely, individuals who disclosed their sexual identity to non-gay individuals tended to have more positive gay identities.

Table 2. *Theories of Gay Identity Development*

	McDonald (1982)	Troiden (1979)	Minton & McDonald (1984)
Stage 1	Awareness	Sensitization	Symbiotic
Stage 2	First gay experience	Dissociation and significance	Sociocentric-objectivistic
Stage 3	Understanding the word "homosexual"	Coming out	Universalistic (acceptance, commitment, and integration of homosexual identity)
Stage 4	Self-labeling	Commitment	
Stage 5	First relationship		
Stage 6	First disclosure to non-gay		
Stage 7	Positive gay identity		

According to McDonald's model, sexual identity development begins with an *awareness* of feelings of same-sex attraction (stage one) and possibly a male's *first homosexual experience* (stage two). After gaining an *understanding of the term "homosexual"* (stage three), he may *self-label* (stage four). This in turn may secure a desire to engage in a *first relationship* (stage five), which may further confirm his identity as a gay male. Once he has made the initial identification as a gay male, he may *first disclose to a heterosexual* (stage six). After a period of time and identity affirming experiences, he may possess a *positive gay identity* (stage seven).

The Troiden Model

Troiden[50] also conducted an empirical study to elucidate factors contributing to a gay male identity. He interviewed 150 gay males to explore how age cohorts, high school heterosexual activity, and high school homosexual activity relate to the pace at which gay identity is acquired. Troiden found that younger respondents tended to report a younger age at which time they (1) thought that they were gay, (2) labeled themselves as gay, and (3) became involved with the gay subculture. Key sequential milestone events facilitating gay male identity began with a *suspicion* that the *individual was homosexual*, which was followed by a *decision to label certain feelings as homosexual*. Soon after, these individuals began to *label themselves as homosexual*, whereby entry into their *first homosexual love relationships* was facilitated. Participants who were older when they identified as gay also reported having more heterosexual experience during high school. For males to identify themselves as "gay," Troiden found that respondents needed to be emotionally ready to self-identify as gay following a period of negative self-perception and self-labeling.

The Minton and McDonald Model

The model proposed by Minton and McDonald[51] utilized Habermas's[52] conceptualization of ego development, that is, the stages of *symbiotic* (lacking identity), *egocentric* (natural identity), *sociocentric-objectivistic* (role identity), and *universalistic* (ego identity) as the framework for homosexual identity development. According to this model, there are two processes to developing a homosexual identity: (1) the formation of a homosexual self-image (i.e., acquiring a homosexual identity) and (2) identity management (i.e., being known publicly as gay). Active completion of these tasks facilitates identity synthesis. By "active completion" we mean that the theorists argue for a "symbolic interactionist position"[53] by which it is assumed that a person actively derives meaning from personal experiences within a social context.

In their analysis of previous models of homosexual identity development, the authors propose a tripartite conceptualization of the process of forming a homosexual self-image: (1) personally interpreting the meaning of homosexual feelings, (2) internalizing society's assumptions of what homosexuality is, and (3) achieving a positive homosexual identity. According to the authors, this tripartite process is well integrated with the Habermas model.

Minton and McDonald's proposed integrative model commences with Habermas's *egocentric* stage because the first phase, *symbiotic*, is merely the recognition that one is different and separate from the environment. In the *egocentric* stage, an individual becomes more aware of the feelings of same-sex attraction, but may not necessarily be cognizant of the label "homosexual" (or the more contemporary label "gay"):

In essence, the first phase of homosexual identity formation involves experiences of an erotic, emotional, or social nature that serves as bases for viewing the self as possibly homosexual. This stage is ego-centric because the individual labels the self as homosexual on the basis of personal experience rather than a normative understanding of homosexuality.[54]

Individuals in the *sociocentric-objectivistic* stage begin to explore the possibility of being homosexual and all that implies according to societal attitudes. This tends to be a variable experience, as "heightened aware-ness provides relief for some individuals; for others it involves anxiety and confusion."[55] The latter experience of confusion is believed by the theorists to be perpetuated by increased homosexual attractions, which leads some individuals to progress towards the advancement of a homo-sexual self. Others may delay or foreclose on their homosexual identities due to defense mechanisms and fears. Minton and McDonald suggest that when an individual has processed through his same-sex attractions and societal assumptions and is ready to "resist outside pressures,"[56] he is then proceeding towards the *universalistic* stage of sexual identity de-velopment.

This last stage, the *universalistic* stage, is designated by the individual's ability to recognize that societal norms and assumptions about homo-sexuality are to be critically evaluated, and as such, the individual can accept and commit to a positive gay identity even though society may condemn it. The authors propose three phases to this final stage: accep-tance of a homosexual identity, commitment to this identity, and integra-tion of this aspect of oneself within the entirety of the self. Identity inte-gration is further enabled by the act of disclosure of one's homosexual identity to other people.

Conclusions on Gay Male Identity Development

Although there are a number of models of gay male sexual identity de-velopment and synthesis, several common threads are noteworthy. For example, the early teen years (coming out stage) are deemed important insofar as feeling different from one's peers is concerned. Troiden's[57] study found that the situation of feeling different occurred at ages 13-17, and McDonald reported awareness of same-sex feelings occurring on average at age 13, and an understanding of the meaning of the word "homosexual" at age 19. Troiden highlighted the significance of the meanings attached to the perceived feelings of difference; this under-scores an important relationship between behavior, attributions or mean-ings, and identity. McDonald noted that same-sex behavior precedes self-identification as a gay male by about 3 years on average. Troiden's sample was similar, in that behavior appears to precede identification: "While commencement of homosexual activity on a regular basis (one or more times per week) is associated with [the coming out] stage . . . a majority of the sample (68%) experienced homosexual contacts to orgasm one or more times prior to labeling themselves as homosexual."[58]

We noted above that one of the first major distinctions in sexual identity theory was based on biological sex. We turn our attention now to models of women's experiences of lesbian sexual identity development and synthesis (see Table 3).

Table 3. *Theories of Lesbian Identity Development*

	Sophie (1986)	Chapman & Brannock (1987)	McCarn & Fassinger (1996)*
Stage 1	First awareness (of homosexual feelings)	Same-sex orientation	Awareness
Stage 2	Testing/exploration	Incongruence	Exploration
Stage 3	Identity acceptance	Self-questioning/ exploration	Deepening/ commitment
Stage 4	Identity integration	Self-identification	Internalization/ synthesis
Stage 5		Choice of lifestyle	

* McCarn and Fassinger have proposed that an individual explores both *individual* sexual identity and *group membership* identity through these same four stages.

Models of Lesbian Identity Development

Models of lesbian identity development arose from the same concern that umbrella models were simply not capturing the experiences of women who experienced same-sex attraction. In fact, models of lesbian sexual identity have generally acknowledged a more variegated experience, one owing perhaps more to external influences that might affect any woman:

> . . . a lesbian identity may, at some point, be a possible outcome for any woman's sexual identity development, whereas biological models . . . restrict lesbian identity to those women who diverge biologically from a heterosexual "norm," or those with an erotic orientation entirely consistent with their sexual identity.[59]

Kitzinger and Wilkinson[60] interviewed 80 lesbians who had spent a minimum of 10 years living heterosexual lives. Sixty-eight percent of these women reported that they had been married prior to their identification as lesbians. In their interviews, Kitzinger and Wilkinson ("Multiple Oppressions" section) reported several recurring themes and attributions of women as they began to experience same-sex behaviors and attractions: "There are multiple oppressions," "I was blocking it out," "We're just good friends," "It's just sex, I was experimenting. Besides, I'm attracted to men too," "It's just a phase," "I'm in love with a person who also happens to be female," "I can't be a lesbian because I cook/ have long hair/have kids/ can't fix my own car," and "She's the lesbian, not me." As they came to understand the narratives presented by these women who had formerly lived heterosexual lives, Kitzinger and Wilkinson found that "[k]ey aspects of developing and maintaining a lesbian self appear to be retrospective accounting ("How did I get to be here?") and future planning ("Where am I going now?")."[61] The notion that a lesbian identity might arise later in life is reiterated in a number of models of lesbian sexual identity development. We will examine a few of these in the pages that follow.

The Sophie Model

Sophie's model[62] is based on themes consistent with previous models of homosexual identity development. The first stage is that of *first awareness* of feelings of same-sex attraction or the relevance of homosexuality to an individual. Consistent with other theories, this first awareness of same-sex attraction precedes contact with other homosexuals and does not result in disclosure of these feelings. The individual might also experience alienation from herself by distancing her emotions, for example, "These feelings are not me."

After a period of time, the individual begins *testing/exploration* her feelings of same-sex attraction by seeking out the homosexual community. If she decides to disclose her feelings of same-sex attraction, there will likely be limited disclosure to heterosexuals. At the same time, while she alienates herself from other heterosexuals, she will refrain from engaging in homosexual relationships due to the newness of these feelings.

The third stage of Sophie's model is *identity acceptance*, in which the individual adopts a lesbian identity; this period of time is characterized by a preference for gay social interactions. Although she might identify as lesbian, the development of a negative lesbian identity precedes a positive identity. Consistent with the previous stage is the limited disclosure of her identity to heterosexuals.

Identity integration is reached when an individual accepts her lesbian identity and integrates it with other aspects in order to create a more stable sense of identity. For some individuals this stage might include a polarizing of the world into gay and straight, resulting in identity pride and anger. At this stage, many people close to the individual who identifies as lesbian are made aware of her sexual identity.

To test this model, which was based on previous models of homosexual identity development, Sophie interviewed 14 women on the topic of sexual orientation issues and found some discrepancies, implying that these stages appeared to be incongruous with the experiences of some lesbians. In her study, some individuals who were in the stage of *first awareness* experienced contact with other lesbians prior to realizing the relevance of homosexuality to themselves. In the *testing/exploration* stage, the experiences of participants contested the presupposition that homosexual relationships did not exist at this stage. Although the theory suggests that lesbians experience a negative identity prior to acquiring a positive one, Sophie found that some participants avoided a negative identity by rejecting the label ("lesbian") until negative consequences disappeared. The last discrepancy between the model and the experiences of the participants was the fact that not all individuals endorsed identity pride and anger as they sought to integrate their sexual identity with other aspects of their identities. Consequently, Sophie observed that:

> We are mistaken if we interpret the notion of stability to mean that individuals who have become lesbian cannot subsequently change. . . . However, the notion has more meaning if we view it as unwillingness to change. . . . The idea of stability has meaning in terms of an increased difficulty in changing toward relations with men among those who have made a commitment to lesbian identity, have been very involved in the lesbian world, and have removed themselves from heterosexual social interactions.[63]

Thus, Sophie's analysis of her model of sexual identity development in lesbians elucidates the variability in the development and timing of events predicted by theories of sexual identity development. The failure of stage theories to predict the course of sexual identity development is what she defines as the "assumption of linearity."[64]

In keeping with other developmental research, the tendency has been to propose stage theories of development of homosexual identity that are inherently linear: Although it is clear that not all who begin at stage one arrive at the final stage of positive gay or lesbian identity, the paths of those who do not proceed through the stages, or who undergo further change after adoption of a gay identity, tend to be ignored.[65]

The Chapman and Brannock Model

This model of lesbian identity development differs from previous models of homosexual identity development in that it asserts that a lesbian identity is present prior to the recognition of the incongruency between lesbians and non-lesbians in their feelings and thoughts.[66] In this model, self-labeling is characterized by two key experiences.

The first key experience occurs through interactions with a non-lesbian world when an individual develops an awareness of some incongruency between her experience and others. For example, if a sophomore in high school realizes that she does not feel the same level of excitement and arousal as her peers, she is more likely than her peers to consider alternatives to the heterosexual norm.

The second experience of self-labeling tends to be a variable process because individuals will assign themselves the label "lesbian" according to perception of experience. Thus, one woman might label herself as lesbian because she has always experienced emotional attractions to women, whereas another woman refers to her experiences as same-sex behaviors.

In addition to these two significant experiences, women who self-identify as lesbian are also believed to go through various stages of sexual identity development. The first stage of this model is *same-sex orientation*, which refers to feeling connected to other females, although the individual may not know the term "lesbian." Soon after, the individual experiences *incongruence* when she realizes that her feelings towards girls and women are different than the attractions other females have. In other words, the feelings of "connection" or wanting to be "connected" to other women may be perceived as different than what other women are believed to experience. Consequently, an individual experiencing this sense of incongruency might also feel isolated and separated from non-lesbian peers, as well as confusion about her lack of desire towards males.

The individual who experiences same-sex attraction starts to think of herself as possibly being lesbian in the third stage of *self-questioning/ exploration.* Her experience of strong emotional bonds with females in combination with strong physical/sexual attractions towards females leads her to begin believing that lesbian feelings are acceptable. However, she may also engage in dating members of the opposite sex as an attempt to figure things out or to try to be heterosexual.

The fourth stage of *self-identification* is delineated by the thought or feeling that "I am lesbian." After this self-labeling, Chapman and Brannock (1987) note that one of two things happens during the fifth stage, *choice of lifestyle*: (1) the individual decides to seek out other females as long-term sexual mates (i.e., identifies as a lesbian through volitional acts of behavior and relationship), or (2) she might decide not to seek other women in long-term sexual relationships although she "maintains" a lesbian sexual orientation. Thus, according to this theory, although she decides not to live her life as a lesbian (i.e., by engaging in behaviors or an intimate same-sex relationship), she is still considered a lesbian because of her emotional attractions to other women.

The McCarn and Fassinger Model

According to McCarn and Fassinger,[67] earlier studies of sexual identity development and synthesis have failed to adequately consider the difference between individual and group aspects of identity, and that these differences may play a role in the formation of a lesbian identity. McCarn and Fassinger believed that certain aspects of female socialization are unique to the formation of a lesbian identity, including "the repression of sexual desire, the interrelationship of intimacy and autonomy, and the recent availability of reinforcement for non-traditional role behavior."[68] In particular, women are also socialized to dismiss their sexual desires and to invalidate those to whom they are attracted (i.e., other women). Consequently, McCarn and Fassinger assert that to capture the development of lesbian identity development adequately, models must consider the importance of intimacy with other women rather than to conceptualize sexual identity formation only in relation to sexual behavior. In their model, two processes are believed to occur: (1) development of a *personal sexual identity*, and (2) understanding of the meaning of *group membership*.

According to the theorists, previous models of sexual identity development tended to conflate the constructs of personal sexual identity and group membership by focusing exclusively or primarily on the development of minority group membership. Consequently, in these models:

> . . . social activism and interpersonal openness are positively associated with mental health and successful internalization of lesbian/gay identity . . . however, the implication that lacking these qualities signals developmental arrest fails to account for the social realities of diverse groups of lesbians and gay men.[69]

Similarly, McCarn and Fassinger viewed previous models of sexual identity development as linear and, as such, they tended ". . . to ignore the paths of those who do not progress predictably through the stages or to view alternative outcomes (bisexuality, heterosexuality) as developmental arrest."[70]

McCarn and Fassinger presented a model of lesbian identity development that conjunctively explores "individual sexual identity" and "group membership identity"; however, these researchers noted that although these two aspects of one's identity progress through the same four stages (*awareness, exploration, deepening/commitment*, and *internalization/synthesis*), they may not occur simultaneously. Thus, a description of the stages of individual sexual identity will be presented first, followed by a description of the group membership identity.

The first stage in this model is a sense of non-awareness of an individual's forthcoming sexual identity or her potential group identity. With *awareness*, the individual realizes that she is different from the heterosexual norm. However, these feelings of same-sex attraction do not necessarily indicate self-labeling as lesbian. In the *exploration* stage, an individual's sexual identity continues to develop as strong/erotic feelings for women are explored, although sexual behavior may not occur. In the third stage, *deepening/commitment*, the individual begins to make a "commitment to self-fulfillment as a sexual being."[71] In addition, intimacy and identity become synthesized—to be intimate implies something about her identity. In the last stage, *internalization/synthesis*, a female's love for women and sexual choices are synthesized into an identity such that, internally, she feels congruent.

In considering group membership identity, the first stage (*awareness*) is defined by the realization that people may experience different sexual orientations. An individual's group membership identity continues to develop in the *exploration* stage, whereby her attitude towards homosexuals as a group changes as she begins to define herself in relation to lesbians. As she begins to deepen her commitment (*deepening/commitment*) to lesbians, she begins to increase her personal involvement with the group and becomes more aware of the oppression of homosexuals. *Internalization and synthesis* of an individual's identity as lesbian commences with her identification as a lesbian in all contexts of her life. Although she may have politicized her awareness of the oppression of lesbians, this is no longer necessary for a woman who has internalized and synthesized her lesbian identity.

Conclusions on Lesbian Identity Development

Although there has generally been less research conducted to date on lesbian sexual identity development, the consensus is that the experience of sexual identity is much morevariegated. The research by Kitzinger and Wilkinson, for example, specifically details the experiences of self-identifying lesbians who had spent many years identifying and living as heterosexual.

Similarly, in Sophie's study,[72] at least at the later stages of identity development, the fluidity of lesbian sexual identity is noted, as three of the 14 women later changed their preferences toward heterosexuality. *What* a particular person experiences as *change*—whether it be, for example, sexual orientation or the broader construct of sexual identity—is open to debate, but we have chosen to focus on the experiences of individuals who participated in our study. We listen to their stories *in their own voices*.

Conclusion

In examining several of the earliest theories of homosexual identity development, followed by several models of gay male and lesbian identity development, we have seen that there is increasing appreciation for the milestone events occurring along the path toward sexual identity synthesis. In fact, some theorists today question whether sexual identity ever really reaches true synthesis. A number of theorists hold that there may indeed be more fluidity to sexual identity than was previously thought, and that this flexibility is particularly salient among women who identity as lesbian.

We turn now to discuss emerging trends in theories of sexual identity development and synthesis. These include heterosexual identity development, bisexual identity development, ethnic minority identity development, and the role of valuative frameworks among those who identify (as well as those who dis-identify) with LGB-affirming ideologies, and the persons and groups supporting such ideologies.

Chapter 2

Emerging Trends in Sexual Identity Theory

Introduction

There are certainly a number of emerging trends in research and theory about sexual identity development; they range from recent models of heterosexual identity development, to criticism of stage theories as too linear and "lock step," to an emphasis on the role of attributions, meaning-making, and valuative frameworks among those who dis-identify with a lesbian, gay, or bisexual (LGB) identity.

We turn our attention first to recent models of heterosexual identity development, followed by a discussion of bisexual identity development and issues confronted by ethnic minorities who experience same-sex attraction. Discussion of emerging trends is followed by an analysis of the experiences of those who dis-identify with gay-affirming ideologies and the individuals and subcultures that embrace such ideologies.

Models of Heterosexual Identity Development

Several LGB theorists argue that heterosexuality is often presumed to be the default sexual orientation due to the perception that people do not necessarily progress through heterosexual identity formation. The assumption is that "You are until you aren't." An attempt to critically evaluate these assumptions and articulate a process of heterosexual identity development has been undertaken most recently by Worthington and his colleagues, and Mohr, whose conceptualizations were inspired by Eliason's study.

The Eliason Model

In one of the first studies of heterosexual identity development, Eliason[1] asked 26 heterosexual students how they arrived at their self-identification. Her results yielded seven common themes, which duplicate Marcia's proposed identity statuses: diffusion, foreclosure, moratorium, and achievement.

One quarter of females and over one third of males stated that they *"had never thought about sexual identity,"*[2] which Eliason suggests is consistent with Marcia's[3] proposed stage of identity diffusion. Over 80% of women and men revealed that some *"outside forces"* [4] shaped their heterosexual identity—an assertion analogous with Marcia's stage of identity foreclosure. Another substantial influence on sexual identity was *"gender socialization,"*[5] which was cited by 42% of women and 38% of men. Twice as many males (36%) compared to females (16%) regarded their "sexuality to be innate,"[6] whereas 8% of females and 7% of males viewed heterosexuality as a choice. Over three times as many males (29%) compared to females (8%) stated that they did not foresee any *"viable options to heterosexuality,"*[7] which Eliason posits is due to the societal stereotype or preconception that to be masculine is equivalent to being heterosexual. Femininity is apparently not as powerfully equated to heterosexuality. One third of women and 43% of men declared that the religious values and beliefs they were raised with as children influenced their heterosexual sexual identities. In her analysis of respondents' commitment to a heterosexual sexual identity, Eliason noted that the majority of males had asserted their heterosexuality because they rejected a gay identity. The female respondents in this study tended not to reject a lesbian identity completely; rather, those who considered a lesbian or bisexual identity at some point decided that their vision of life was better suited to a heterosexual sexual identity.

The Worthington, Savoy, Dillon, and Vernaglia Model

Worthington and his colleagues[8] proposed that one of the major weaknesses of previous models of heterosexuality has been the tendency to focus on sexual orientation as the delineating factor in sexual identity, while precluding "biopsychosocial influences" as factors, and excluding social influences on identity development. Consequently, they proposed that heterosexual identity develops via ". . . the individual and social processes by which heterosexually identified persons acknowledge and define their sexual needs, values, sexual orientation and preferences for sexual activities, modes of sexual expression, and characteristics of sexual partners." Included in this definition is the authors' assumption that individuals undergoing this process are also aware of their status as members in an "oppressive majority group," which accords particular attitudes, values, and beliefs towards sexual minority group members.

The model proposed by Worthington et al. is similar to that of McCarn and Fassinger (who discussed individual and group membership identity) insofar as it features two parallel processes: (1) *individual* sexual identity development in reference to the development (i.e., the "recognition, acceptance of, and identification")[9] of different aspects, such as ". . . sexual needs, values, sexual orientation and preferences for activities, partner characteristics, and modes of sexual expression,"[10] and (2) *social* identity development, which involves the recognition that, as a member of the majority group, an individual subscribes to "group membership identity," which directs certain attitudes towards sexual minorities.

These two parallel processes (i.e., individual and social sexual identity development) transpire within five identity statuses: (1) *unexplored commitment*, (2) *active exploration*, (3) *diffusion*, (4) *deepening and commitment*, and (5) *synthesis*.[11] Worthington et al. emphasized that there "are opportunities for circularity and revisiting of statuses throughout the lifespan development of any given individual."[12]

Unexplored commitment—with respect to individual sexual identity—is thought to be characterized by the lack of conscious thought towards what Worthington et al. refer to as the "adoption of compulsory heterosexuality,"[13] which is largely enacted by prepubescent children. Lack of awareness of one's membership in what Worthington et al. portray as a privileged, oppressive majority group, is also thought to define individuals in this stage of social sexual identity development. Majority views are therefore hypothesized to be "repressed . . . or accepted without question as normal, understandable, and justifiable."[14]

In individual sexual identity development, those who pursue *active exploration* are thought to perform purposeful exploration of their "sexual needs, values, orientation and/or preferences for activities, partner characteristics, or modes of sexual expression."[15] *Active exploration* is not merely "naïve behavioral experimentation,"[16] but tends to be intentional cognitive or behavioral exploration, which is purposeful and goal-directed. Thus, in contrast to "normative exploration," which is deemed a function of "uncontrollable maturational processes," active exploration occurs when an individual engages in "cognitive or behavioral exploration of individual sexual identities beyond that which is socially mandated within one's social context."[17] Worthington et al. have conceptualized two trajectories, which follow active exploration: *Deepening/ commitment* or *diffusion*. According to the theorists, members of the majority group either begin to question their privileged status, or else they start to exert their "authority" as privileged members. Thus, between—but also within—members of the majority group, there is likely to be a wide variation of attitudes towards sexual minorities.

The identity status of *diffusion* is thought to be characterized by the absence of intentional, goal-directed behavior. According to the theorists, individuals are likely to experience "crisis" or "confusion" in some aspect of their lives, which leads them to reject other social and cultural perspectives on identity, behaviors and values. This is not a purposeful rejection; rather, it is the confusion and resultant lack of awareness and understanding that leads someone to "reject" these other points of view. This "rejection" extends into their sexual lives and restricts their identity. In keeping with this view, it is only through active exploration that an individual can move beyond the identity status of diffusion.

In contrast to *diffusion*, the *deepening/commitment* experience corresponds to increased commitment towards various aspects of an individual's sexual identity (i.e., values, sexual orientation, etc.). Worthington et al. conjectured that this identity status may occur without active exploration due to the functions of maturational development and the consequential changes in unintentional or unexplored thoughts, feelings and behavior. Worthington et al. hypothesized three likely pathways for individual sexual identity development emerging from the *deepening and commitment* status: (1) *synthesis*, or reversions to (2) *active exploration*, and (3) *diffusion*. With regard to social sexual identity development, the attitudes and identity as a majority group member are believed to become more coherent; whereas conceptualizations of the relationships between majority and minority members as more or less privileged/oppressed, respectively, become conscious.

In the final identity status, *synthesis*, individuals are said to experience coherence and congruence between individual and group sexual identity development and the attitudes they espouse towards sexual minority group members. Worthington et al. assert that the only identity status leading to *synthesis* is *deepening and commitment*, in which individuals begin to incorporate other aspects of their personhood through the process of *active exploration*.

The Mohr Model

The Worthington et al. model of conceptualizing heterosexual identity helped to circumscribe the role of a heterosexual therapist in relation to either helping or hindering lesbian, gay or bisexual clients as they sort through their own issues of sexual identification. Mohr[18] went further to define *heterosexual identity* as being different from *heterosexuality* in that it is the "understanding that individuals have of their sexual orientation rather than the sexual orientation itself," including how ". . . perceptions individuals hold of themselves as people whose romantic/sexual attractions, fantasies, and behavior are directed toward people of the opposite sex."[19]

Heterosexual identity is theorized to consist of both personal and public facets. A personal heterosexual identity is the individual's "inner experience and understanding of their heterosexual orientation,"[20] whereas the same individual's public heterosexual identity refers to interpersonal interactions as manifested by expression, presentation, and assertion of heterosexual experiences.

Mohr's model comprises three groups of influences of adult heterosexual identity. They are: (1) *precursors of adult heterosexual identity*, (2) *determinants of heterosexual identity*, and (3) *determinants of identity states*.

Precursors of adult heterosexual identity include "experiences with personal sexuality," such as sexual experiences, sexual attractions and sexual fantasies, as well as "exposure to social information about sexual orientation,"[21] which would include familial members, peers, media, community institutions (e.g., school, church) and so on, that provide social meaning to the experience of one's attractions.

Mohr proposed two *determinants of adult heterosexual identity*: "working models of sexual orientation" and "core motivations."[22] Mohr used the term "working model" to conceptualize the framework through which individuals understand their own sexual orientation and that of others. Various experiences pertaining to personal sexuality are thought to combine with exposure to social information about sexual orientation; they work together to create internal working models, which guide one's anticipation, interpretation and response to information on sexual orientation.

Mohr's first working model is "democratic heterosexuality," which considers sexual orientation as "an expression of individual difference . . . but not of fundamental significance."[23] Individuals who subscribe to this working model are believed to detect differences related to sexual attraction; however, they are also thought to regard everyone as essentially the same. According to the model, there is a tendency for these individuals to live out their heterosexuality without any self-exploration whatsoever, especially given the possibility that they may, at some point, experience same-sex attraction. These individuals might be at risk, in that they may assume that differences in sexual orientation do not contribute to meaningful life experiences . . . as a direct result of that dissimilarity. Mohr categorizes these individuals as prone to ignorance or reductionistic thinking with regard to privilege and the subsequent consequences for sexual minority group members. According to Mohr, certain limitations experienced by therapists who may tend towards democratic views of heterosexuality include assumptions that all clients are heterosexual; they may lack knowledge of the negative effects of social heterosexism and homophobia on clients; and they may ignore their own susceptibility to stereotypes and heterosexism.

The second working model presented by Mohr is "compulsory heterosexuality," which considers heterosexuality as the only morally and socially acceptable form of sexual orientation, because all other variations of sexual orientation "threaten core value systems."[24] Therapists who endorse this working model are said to not interact with gay and lesbian identified clients whom they are likely to believe have contravened important norms and standards of behavior. In therapy, these therapists may view non-heterosexuality as a type of disorder and subscribe to stereotypes of gay and lesbian individuals.

The third working model proposed by Mohr is referred to as "politicized heterosexuality."[25] This model is said to emphasize the oppressed and underprivileged existence of gay and lesbian clients. Individuals within this category are thought to dichotomize views of sexual orientation: one is either homophobic or gay affirmative. A "politicized" heterosexual therapist may be prone to impatience with clients who express difficulty accepting non-heterosexuality, including those with same-sex attraction but who are experiencing internalized homophobia. According to Mohr, these therapists might also mistakenly overemphasize issues of sexual orientation in gay and lesbian identified clients, encourage these clients to "come out" to important people in their lives without necessarily considering any negative outcomes, and idealize these clients.

The last working model of Mohr is that of "integrative heterosexuality,"[26] which portrays sexual orientation as a multidimensional continuum and acknowledges the societal constraints placed on all members of society, regardless of individual sexual orientation.

In addition to working models, "core motivations" are also determinants of heterosexual identity. Mohr identifies two categories of motivations: those related to a need for acceptance from social reference groups, and those which help to develop an internally consistent and non-ambiguous sense of oneself. The latter core motivation indicates that individuals will feel driven to have congruent public and private identities.

Mohr described the interplay between "core motivations" and "working models" as synergistic in the development of a heterosexual identity:

> To satisfy the core motivations, individuals will gravitate toward the use of a working model of sexual orientation that is congruent with other aspects of their identity and allows them to fit in with their social reference groups.[27]

The dynamic interaction between core motivations and working models facilitates yet another process Mohr describes as "identity states," which are variable and dependent on context. However, Mohr claims they are usually called into action to attenuate feelings of tension and increase feelings of comfort and self-worth.

Theories of heterosexual identity development are clearly in their infant stages, and as researchers conduct empirical studies, the findings should provide us with a greater understanding of how the vast majority of persons across cultures come to identify as heterosexual in their sexual identity synthesis. We turn now to another emerging trend in sexual identity theory, that is, bisexual identity development.

Bisexual Identity Development

According to bisexual identity theorists, bisexuality is a complex sexual identification that may depend on situations and circumstances.[28] Bisexuality may be a transitional stage in the process of coming out as gay or lesbian (or vice versa), or historical, in that an individual who presently identifies as heterosexual or homosexual may have had same- or opposite-sex attractions in the past. Likewise, some individuals have sequential bisexual relationships, that is, either a male or female relationship at a time, whereas other individuals experience concurrent relationships with men and women. Bisexual behavior may also be reported as a product of a culture, or an environmental circumstance when there is limited access to heterosexual relationships.

As with heterosexual identity development, there are relatively few theories and empirical studies on bisexual identity development.[29] However, previous theories of how homosexual identity develops have created a niche, which facilitates the conceptualization of theories of bisexual identity development:

> . . . the emergence of lesbian and gay identity theory represented an important shift in emphasis in developmental theory, away from the concern with etiology and psychopathology characteristic of the illness model toward articulation of the factors involved in the formation of positive gay and lesbian identities.[30]

In other words, previous theories of sexual identity development have led to the conceptualization of sexual orientation from a multidimensional perspective that includes emotional and social preferences, self-identification, sexual attraction, sexual behavior, fantasy, and fluid sexual identities.

The Fox Model

Consistent with these insights, Fox has developed a "multidimensional theoretical approach" of bisexual identity development, which highlights the variation of the process by which bisexual individuals attain their sexual identity. In addition, Fox's model recognizes the influences of personal and social factors that may maintain or alter a bisexual individual's sexual identity.

In the initial stage of the Fox model, early adolescents experience their *first heterosexual attractions, behaviors and relationships*. The *first homosexual attractions, behaviors and relationships* are thought to occur in early to middle adolescence for males and late adolescence for females. Both males and females tend to experience their first homosexual relationship in their early 20s. According to Fox, bisexual males and females tend to *initially self-identify as bisexual* in late adolescence/young adulthood, which is a few years after gay males and females. Soon after, individuals who conceive themselves to be bisexual *self-disclose* their identities to others. In contemplating the actual experiences of bisexual males and females, Fox notes that most bisexual women experience heterosexual attractions and behavior prior to their first homosexual attractions and behavior. More bisexual men experience homosexual attractions and behaviors earlier or at the same time as their heterosexual attractions and behaviors. Consequently, there is no single pattern of bisexual identity development via homosexual and heterosexual attractions and behaviors.

The Weinberg, Williams and Pryor Model

Another model of bisexual identity development was proposed by Weinberg, Williams and Pryor.[31] According to these researchers, "Becoming bisexual involves the rejection of not one but two recognized categories of sexual identity: heterosexual and homosexual."[32] The first three stages of their model (*initial confusion, finding and applying the label*, and *settling into the identity*) are similar to models of development for gay and lesbian individuals. The last stage, *continued uncertainty*, is believed to be experientially unique to individuals who claim a bisexual orientation.

The first stage, *initial confusion*, often occurs when individuals become aware of attraction to both same and opposite sex members, and consequently experience feelings of doubt, confusion and tension. The confusion may be related to a number of different incidences: feeling as if they cease to be heterosexual because of same-sex attractions, inability to categorize feelings and sexual behaviors, and homophobia. Due to the paucity of information available about bisexuality, denial of their sexual attractions is believed to be due to fear of the meaning of these experiences.

In an effort to understand the meaning of being attracted to both same and opposite sex members, individuals concerned must first decide whether they want to explore their bisexual attractions. A juncture of this kind is indicative of the stage of *finding and applying the label*, which for many is a turning point, a realization that this category of sexual identity exists. Other factors influencing the decision to explore bisexuality include the recognition that one may undergo immense difficulty in denying same- and opposite-sex attractions, and also receiving the support of

others. However, according to the theorists, not everyone inclined towards bisexuality decides to explore it; the cost of this attempt may be
too great, and is thus never attempted. Those who do investigate their
inclinations can struggle with issues of loyalty, not only to a current
partner but also to the category of men or women. In other words, they
may struggle with loyalty to their sexual identity. In this model, it is
understood as an ideological, emotional, and relational state of distress
for a person who at one time had thought his or her sexual identity to be
determined (e.g., a male who has considered identification as gay may
find opposite-sex attraction to be somewhat overwhelming in light of the
fact that he has already begun to identify as a particular sexual minority).
Once the decision is made to pursue a bisexual identity, the process of
identification follows that of achieving a gay or lesbian identity: engagement in a relationship, finding a community, and disclosing to significant
others.

The third stage proposed by Weinberg et al. is *settling into the identity*, a stage characterized by greater self-acceptance of one's sexual identity
as bisexual and decreased preoccupation with the opinions of others about
sexuality. Although the majority of the respondents in the study reported
not being in transition to homosexuality or heterosexuality, a proportion
did acknowledge that they would define themselves as either heterosexual
or homosexual were they to enter into a monogamous or intensely meaningful relationship. That a large portion of the bisexual respondents in
this study still experienced some doubt about their identities as bisexuals
is also noteworthy. Their doubt intensified when they experienced strong
attraction to members of the sex opposite to that of their current partner.
Thus, despite their self-acceptance, a proportion of bisexual individuals
are believed to experience little closure with respect to their sexual
identities.

Continued uncertainty, the final stage of Weinberg et al.'s model, is
characterized by what the theorists believe is lingering doubt: "even after having discovered and applied the label 'bisexual' to themselves, and
having come to the point of apparent self-acceptance, they still experienced continued intermittent periods of doubt and uncertainty regarding
their sexual identity."[33] Several reasons are given by the theorists, including the perceived rejection, judgment, and prejudice directed against
bisexuals by gays and lesbians (as well as heterosexuals), the lack of
bisexual role models, an inability to synthesize same-sex attractions into
same-sex behaviors, feelings of doubt about a bisexual identity because

of engagement in an either exclusive heterosexual or homosexual relationship, and unequal sexual attractions to both same- and opposite-sex partners.

Conclusions on Bisexual Identity Development

Although there has been relatively little research on the experiences of individuals who identify as bisexual, recent discussions have uncovered a possible developmental pathway toward a bisexual identity. However, these discussions are not without controversy, since some theorists argue that bisexuality represents a coming out as lesbian or gay stage, while others insist that bisexuality as an identity occurs after coming out as either lesbian or gay.[34]

Exploration of the notion of a sexual identity continuum (heterosexual, bisexual, homosexual—not as discrete categories but as a continuum of sexual attraction) may provide evidence of the plasticity of sexual feelings for certain persons: ". . . self-ratings of sexual attraction, fantasy, and behavior may vary significantly for bisexual individuals *and* for lesbian, gay, and heterosexual individuals and that ratings on these factors, including self-identification, change over time."[35]

We next turn to ethnic minority sexual identity development. In response to the extant literature, many ethnic minority persons who also identified as LGB did not recognize their experiences in the current theories proposed to date.

Ethnic Minority Sexual Identity Development

Sexual minorities often report feeling marginalized in society. Ethnic minorities report similar feelings. As marginalized members of society, ethnic sexual minority individuals undergo a fairly strenuous process of definition and identification distinct from that presumed of individuals in dominant culture. However, the complexity of identification as LGB is thought to be even more pronounced when an ethnic minority individual is trying to comprehend having membership in both minority groups.[36] According to Savin-Williams, ethnic minority and sexual minority-identifying youth:

> Often feel that they must choose which of the two groups will be their primary identification. Coupled with conflicting pressures from peers

and the mass media to assimilate by acting White and heterosexual, youths from ethnic communities who are gay, bisexual, or lesbian struggle between who they are and that which they feel they must be in order to avoid a stigmatizing identity.[37]

Integration of sexual and ethnic minority identities into a wholesome sense of self therefore becomes an emotional and relationship-challenging task.

The Ritter and Terndrup Model

Ritter and Terndrup[38] recently compared the various stages of sexual minority identity development and ethnic minority identity development.[39] Ritter and Terndrup conceptualized five phases of sexual minority identity development they believe run parallel to the five stages of minority identity development: *conformity, dissonance, resistance and immersion, introspection,* and *synergetic articulation and awareness.*

The first phase of either sexual or ethnic minority identity development is characterized by an overidentification with the dominant group, which leads these individuals to "unconsciously devalue themselves."[40] Although there is the proclivity for acting in accordance with perceived White, heterosexual norms, these individuals still feel socially different, which is hypothesized to further perpetuate and exacerbate their anxiety.

Individuals in the second phase of sexual identity formation begin to notice that they feel different from others sexually and consider the possibility of being gay, lesbian, or bisexual. These prospective labels and identities elicit shameful internal conflicts. Likewise, ethnic minorities experience shame when they recognize the racial/ethnic/cultural differences which distinguish them from the dominant group in the *conformity* stage of minority identity development. At this point, these individuals continue to overvalue dominant culture and simultaneously dismiss their minority cultures.

The internal experience of the third and fourth phases of sexual minority identity development appear to be similar to the *dissonance* stage of minority identity development: the awareness that the dominant culture's values are not necessarily beneficial for minority group members. Consequently, members of an ethnic minority group begin to vacillate between pride and shame at having membership in an ethnic group. In phase three of sexual minority identity development, ethnic minority group members who experience same-sex attraction are thought to explore their emotional, social and sexual needs *after* realizing that the dominant culture is not validating either their ethnic or their sexual differences. Meanwhile, they are thought to be learning increasingly about their cultural heritage. A sense of pride is then thought to emerge. However, according to the theorists, most individuals attempting to balance these two minority cultural identities ". . . devote most of their energy during this phase to reconciling conflicts within themselves and with their majority and minority cultures."[41] Phase four is thought to be characterized by an abatement of feelings of dissonance between pride and shame as these individuals begin to accept their sexual and ethnic identities.

The authors hypothesize that Cass's stage of *identity pride* and Atkinson et al.'s *resistance and immersion* stages are "virtually parallel processes"[42] as individuals become increasingly proud of their ethnic and sexual minority identities and immerse themselves in these minority cultures while distancing themselves from dominant culture's heterosexism and racism. However, when nearing the end of these stages, it is believed that these individuals realize that differences exist within their sexual and ethnic minority cultures, and that they indeed share certain similarities with the dominant culture. An *awareness/introspection* (minority identity development) leads these individuals to integrate their multiple minority identities as they become more uncomfortable having such a dichotomous view of the world.

Synergistic articulation and awareness in minority identity development is believed to coincide with the end of the fifth phase of sexual minority identity development as these individuals integrate their multiple identities into a "singular, multifaceted self-concept,"[43] which appreciates individuals, regardless of sexual or ethnic identity. This "awareness" is attributed to a shift in perception in which they perceive that others recognize their humanity, and are not merely sympathetic to a shared sexual orientation or ethnicity. Paramount to this process of integration is the abandonment of previously held dichotomous beliefs about the nature of their identification (e.g., ethnic minority identity versus White; LGB versus heterosexual).

The Morales Model

Morales[44] proposed a model of sexual and ethnic identity integration focusing on the discordant feelings experienced by ethnic minority gay, lesbian, and bisexual individuals as they integrate two or more seemingly divisive cultural realities. The five states (versus "stages" due to the cognitive and emotional malleability of the internal and cognitive processes involved) in the Morales model are: *denial of conflicts, bisexual versus gay or lesbian, conflicts in allegiances, establishing priorities in allegiance,* and *integrating the various communities.*

In the first state, *denial of conflicts,* individuals tend to have an over-idealistic and utopian view of reality with the notion that their own sexual orientation does not impact other areas of their lives.[45] These individuals also tend not to be accurate in their assessment of racial discrimination as a real occurrence.

Individuals in the second state assume a *bisexual versus gay or lesbian* identity in order to evade being labeled by their ethnic community; concurrently, these individuals avoid the gay or lesbian community, which they assume as part of "White racist society."[46] In this state, sexual attraction—regardless of the sex of the person to whom one is attracted—is indicative of sexuality.

Conflicts in allegiances is characterized by feeling "torn" between choosing one's ethnic minority group and the gay, lesbian, and bisexual community. Both these groups are oppressed by the dominant culture, but one is indecisive about aligning oneself with either group.

The fourth state, *establishing priorities in allegiance,* is characterized by feelings of anger, resentment, and frustration caused by the exclusivity of different communities (ethnic versus gay, lesbian, or bisexual) in which an individual takes part.[47] These negative feelings might stem from experiences of racism within the sexual minority community as well as exclusion of significant others—of a different ethnicity—from one's own ethnic community.

In the last stage, individuals attempt to *integrate the various communities* (i.e., ethnic and sexual minority) in which they participate; however, the process is difficult and often fraught with anxiety, frustration and alienation at the limitations they perceive in the duration. Individuals may feel compelled to bridge the two communities despite ongoing conflicts of allegiance.

Theories of ethnic minority experiences with LGB identity development draw heavily on existing models of ethnic minority identity development. The challenge here involves sorting out the myriad ways to relate ethnic and sexual minority communities. Again, as an emerging area in sexual identity theory, there is ample opportunity for researchers and theorists to analyze the complexities of these issues.

One particularly interesting issue, which may have developed partly from the difficulties encountered by ethnic minority persons with same-sex attractions, is how one's beliefs and values (or valuative framework) may conflict with acting on or identifying with same-sex attraction (as a "gay identity"). We turn now to the role of valuative frameworks, attribution, and meaning-making in identifying and dis-identifying with LGB-affirming ideologies and the people and groups supporting such ideologies.

Identification/Dis-Identification with LGB-Affirming Ideology

There have been calls for a more inclusive response to individuals who experience same-sex attraction and who choose to either integrate experiences of same-sex attraction into an LGB identity or dis-identify with a personal or group membership identity.[48]

Although Beckstead's[49] model is not specifically a model of sexual identity development, it is a summons for a new approach to interventions, thus a broadening of the "change of orientation" debate. In his empirical work in this area, he finds that those fare better—whether involved in LGB-affirmative or sexual reorientation approaches—tend to (a) spend time with like-minded others, (b) participate in a small group for support, (c) de-stigmatize the experience of same-sex attraction, (d) experience an increase in autonomy and self-determination, (e) increase their comfort with their gender role, and (f) experience increased family and peer group support.

The commonly shared view of many of the models of LGB identity development is the assumption that successful sexual identity synthesis is achieved when an individual integrates experience of same-sex attraction into a LGB identity. Although there may be a few exceptions to the norm, most models hold that normal same-sex identity development propels the individual toward an integrated LGB self-identification. From this perspective, "coming out" as LGB (and making the self-defining attribution, "I am gay") is treated as synonymous to healthy sexual identity synthesis. This appears to leave little room for those who dis-identify with LGB-affirming ideologies and the individuals and organizations supporting such ideologies.

In their review of the sexual and ethnic identity literature, McCarn and Fassinger[50] noted that existing models of sexual identity development tend to view "alternative outcomes," such as heterosexuality, as "developmental arrest" for gays or lesbians. In their critique the authors pave the way towards understanding sexual identity development which might help theorists account for experiences of those who dis-identify with an LGB-affirming ideology and who achieve an alternative sexual identity synthesis.

In an attempt to account for those who dis-identify with an LGB-affirming ideology, Yarhouse[51] offers an alternative theory of sexual identity development and synthesis. He points out that chastity or celibacy are shunned by many sexual identity theorists, who identify attempts at abstaining from same-sex relationships despite having these feelings, as "denial or worse."[52] In previous discussions regarding the role of religion in sexual identity development, emphasis has been on changing sexual orientation, rather than the experience of "dis-identification" (i.e., choosing not to identify as LGB despite experiences of same-sex attraction), which an individual having same-sex attractions might consider because of personal or religion-informed values.

The Yarhouse Model

Yarhouse proposes that a personal and/or religious valuative framework may affect sexual identity development at the level of attributions that an individual makes concerning sexual identity. These attributions may deal with the meaning of same-sex attraction ("Are these attractions signaling who I 'really am' as a person?"), as well as choosing what to do with one's experiences of same-sex attraction ("I have a choice between acting on them and facilitating my sexual identity or pursuing chastity or some other behavior.").

The first stage of the Yarhouse model of sexual identity synthesis resembles most models: *Identity confusion or crisis*. The individual is thought to experience confusion due to feeling same-sex attraction. Although not the case for everyone, for some, feelings of confusion may lead to an identity crisis if those experiences of same-sex attraction are discordant with the individual's own values, beliefs or religion. Thus, according to this model, the occurrence of an identity crisis might be due to the attributions an individual makes regarding the meaning of experiences of same-sex attraction.

This brings the individual into the second stage of this model: *Identity attribution*. At this point, some may attribute experiences of same-sex attraction as indicative of a gay or lesbian identity, that is, they think that same-sex attraction signals who they "really are" as a person. Others however, may attribute feelings of same-sex attraction to a "proclivity or inclination" without subscribing to a personal gay identity. Thus, how one explains experiences of same-sex attraction to oneself may factor significantly in the decision to identify (personally and through group membership) as LGB.

After making attributions regarding the meaning of experiences of same-sex attraction, the belief is that an individual may pursue a gay or lesbian identity or explore other possible identities. This is the *identity foreclosure versus expansion* stage. According to Yarhouse, individuals who adopt an LGB identity undergo the same stages described by Cass, Troiden and other theorists. By following this trajectory, the implication is that an LGB identity is facilitated by increased social contact with others who identify as LGB.

Individuals who experience same-sex attraction but do not adopt either a personal or group identity as LGB for any number of reasons, including their own valuative framework, nevertheless seek to expand their identity. The experience of identity expansion is sometimes organized around an individual's emphasis on biological sex (as male or female), gender identity (of being masculine or feminine), or religious identity (e.g., a Christian who experiences identity as "in Christ"). Identity expansion is not simply the pursuit of an alternative set of behaviors, but rather is indicative of the search for a broader and deeper personal and public identity.

The fourth stage of this model is *identity reappraisal*. According to Yarhouse, Tan, and Pawlowski,[53] when one encounters difficulties that lead to dissatisfaction with either "identification" (with LGB-affirming ideologies and individuals/subcultures that subscribe to them) or "dis-identification" with the same, one may re-consider the decision (hence, make a reappraisal). Dissatisfaction with an initial decision to identify or dis-identify with LGB-affirming ideologies and so on may lead one to the first stage of *identity confusion or crisis*. At this time, the "crisis they face is that their efforts have failed with respect to either organizing their sense of identity around their experience of same-sex attraction or around efforts to change these impulses."[54] Thus, they experience a sense of crisis: how can they understand their feelings of same-sex attraction now? Altogether, these experiences and attempts at meaning-making become key to the experience of sexual identity development.

If individuals had experienced satisfaction with their choice of identifying or dis-identifying with lesbian, gay, and bisexual-affirming ideologies and so on during the *identity reappraisal* stage, they will proceed to consolidate their sexual identity—either as someone who identifies as gay or lesbian, or as an individual who struggles with same-sex attraction, but does not label oneself according to the experience of same-sex attraction. These scenarios indicate that the person is entering the final stage of identity development, *identity synthesis*.

One of the strengths of this model is its consideration of diverse experience within the community of individuals who experience same-sex attraction—whether they identify as lesbian, gay, or bisexual or whether they dis-identify with lesbian, gay, and bisexual-affirming ideologies. Interestingly, there is no attempt to negate assertions of previous models concerning specific meanings of the stages; rather, this model provides an adjunctive level of considerations while working with clients who experience same-sex attraction—that is, the role that personal and/ or religious valuative frameworks might play in the process of personal and group membership identification.

Conclusion

There are several emerging trends in theories of sexual identity development. We have discussed heterosexual identity development, ethnic minority sexual identity development, and the role of valuative frameworks and attributions among those who identity and dis-identity with LGB-affirming ideologies; it is this last emerging trend that will be explored further in this volume. We will now discuss the larger study of key milestone events perceived by individuals who have or currently experience same-sex attraction and who currently identify as either LGB, or who have dis-identified with an LGB identity and LGB-affirming ideology.

Part 2

The Sexual Identity Project

Chapter 3

The Population and Study

Introduction

Encompassed in the comprehensive notion of sexuality is the more specific idea of sexual identity. We have suggested that one's sexual identity is a complex construct comprised of, among other things, biological sex as male or female, sense of gender as masculine or feminine, experiences of sexual and affectional attraction, and behaviors as expressions of sexual attractions, as well as values and intentions that regulate that behavior. Thus, an individual's sexual identity is fairly complex, and may be influenced to varying degrees by peers, environment, religious or personal values, and so on.

We have found in research and clinical experience that, among those who feel same-sex attraction, certain individuals identify with their attraction to the same sex and therefore integrate their experiences into a lesbian, gay, or bisexual (LGB) identity synthesis; whereas other individuals dis-identify with their experiences of same-sex attraction, including the people and organizations that promote a gay-affirming ideology.

Those who integrate their experiences of same-sex attraction into an LGB identity synthesis often describe their sexual preference towards members of the same sex as reflecting an aspect of themselves as persons. Although they may also be religious, they privilege their LGB identity over specific religious teachings in part because they declare that to do otherwise is to deny their authenticity.[1] Erin Blades shares her experience of a lesbian identity synthesis and how her identity as lesbian surpasses mere sexual behavior:

> When I say I'm gay, I'm not just talking about who I sleep with. It's not what I do, it's how I am. It's so much more than sex. Even outside the bedroom my identity as a lesbian colors every aspect of my life. If people weren't so concerned about sex (especially homosexual sex), we wouldn't be hunting for the gay gene.[2]

In contrast to this experience of an LGB identity synthesis, we have mentioned that an unknown percentage of individuals who experience same-sex attraction choose to dis-identify with their attractions. They might describe themselves as *contending* with same-sex attraction, who rather than integrate their attractions into an LGB identity synthesis, dis-identify with their attractions and with the broader LGB community. Although there is debate about whether a percentage of these individuals detect shifts in their sexual orientation (referring more specifically to persistence and direction of sexual attractions),[3] they report at least a change in sexual identity with respect to their self image both privately and publicly.

Among those who are religiously affiliated, they appear to prioritize their religious identity and the beliefs and valuative frameworks attending to that religion. Consequently, despite attraction towards the same sex, they choose their religious beliefs as the demarcation of their identity. Andrew Comisky[4] captured something of this experience when he wrote, "Intense sexual feeling cannot alone determine what is basically true about one's sexuality and one's humanity in general."

We have addressed our questions about sexual identity to these two groups of people. Our questions were posed in order to better understand the relationship between sexual identity and a valuative framework, particularly that of Christianity, which, throughout history, has viewed same-sex behavior as immoral. Our guiding research questions have been, "What are the stories of these two groups of individuals? How did they come to identify either as LGB and Christian, or Christian despite same-sex attraction?" We aimed to learn the major milestones in these journeys of identification as well as the similarities and differences.

In research, the fewer confounding or potentially influential variables there are, the better. Thus, we decided to seek Christian participants who identified as LGB, and those who did not identify, that is, who *dis*-identified. We chose Christianity as our religious focus simply because it remains the majority religion (by self-identification) in the United States (US). Similar studies can and have been done with other religious groups.[5]

As we have suggested, in an attempt to reduce the factors that might account for differences between our samples, we sought self-identifying Christian communities, that is, groups of individuals who experience same-sex attraction and who identify publicly as Christian. In so doing we identified communities that either affirmed a gay identity or facilitated what we refer to as the dis-identification with an LGB identity. This approach is consistent with the ethnographic research by Wolkomir,[6] who interviewed 16 participants from the Universal Fellowship Metropolitan Community Church (UFMCC) and 14 participants in Exodus North America support groups. Consistent with Wolkomir's findings, the majority of our participants were raised in conservative Christian communities in which sexual behavior was tied to transcendent meaning. For example, sex between a man and a woman in marriage was seen as instructive insofar as it points to the transcendent meaning of the relationship between Christ and the Church, often referred to as "the Bride of Christ"). From this perspective, fidelity in marriage and chastity outside of marriage is normative.

We turn our attention now to descriptions of both the UFMCC and Exodus North America. These were the organizations we contacted to help us identify potential participants for our study.

The Universal Fellowship of Metropolitan Community Churches

History of UFMCC

Reverend Troy D. Perry was 27 years old at the time he founded the first UFMCC located in Los Angeles, California in 1968. Rev. Perry says he realized at age 13 that he was called to become a pastor and within two years, he obtained his license as a Baptist minister. During the time he was married with children, Rev. Perry became more attuned to his feelings of same-sex attraction. The disclosure of this information led to a divorce and estrangement from his children, in addition to his removal as a minister and the loss of his license. The combination of separation and stress led to a failed suicide attempt; however, upon recovery, Rev. Perry continued to believe that God's love and promises were available to all, regardless of sexual orientation. Thus, he felt called to start a church that did not reject, but instead welcomed members of society on the fringe—gays, lesbians, and others who were left out by the main-stream churches. On October 6, 1968, Rev. Perry gathered with 11 men and one woman for the first worship service in what would later become the Metropolitan Community Church of Los Angeles, CA. These first 12 congregants were considered as the predecessors of future congregations because of the diverse quality of the group: members of Protestant, Catholic and Jewish institutions, one heterosexual couple, an individual of Jewish descent, and one Latino individual.

Taking an emic perspective, a view from within this particular gay community, the UFMCC represents a place of spiritual nurturing and has played an important role providing support to various gay and lesbian organizations and projects internationally. As an advocate for civil and human rights, especially those pertaining to perceived mistreatment of individuals based on sexual orientation, UFMCC has campaigned against religious right-wing extremists, bans against gays and lesbians in the military, violations of human rights internationally, and has promoted anti-discrimination laws in five continents: North and South America, Asia, Europe, and Africa. UFMCC is also a very high profile advocate in the fight for funding to serve people affected by HIV and AIDS by providing education, as well as resources to offer medical care to those afflicted in their communities. However, UFMCC's attempts to endorse religious and sexual integration have not been without consequences. Between 1971 and 1985, 18 churches reported to have been victims of arson. Threats of violence against UFMCC persist today.

Since its inception in 1968, UFMCC has become a worldwide denomination with a membership of over 40,000 congregants in 18 countries. For many who struggle with reconciling faith with sexual identity, UFMCC is often regarded as the only gay, lesbian or bisexually affirming advocate, which supports and attends to individuals' spiritual needs.

Tenets of UFMCC

The UFMCC seeks to help gay, lesbian, bisexual, and transgendered (GLBT) identified people with their spiritual needs in an attempt to reconcile their earlier harmful experiences with the religious institutions that had inflicted shame and guilt onto them because of same-sex attraction or behavior. Those who have found a spiritual connection through UFMCC claim that, "Today, as self-aware and self-affirming gay men and lesbians, we reclaim the fullness of our humanity, including our spirituality. We find great truths in the religious tradition, and we find that our encounter with God is transformational and healing" (www.mccchurch.org). Their mission statement reads:

> The Universal Fellowship of Metropolitan Community Churches is a Christian Church founded in and reaching beyond the Gay and Lesbian Communities. We embody and proclaim Christian salvation and liberation, Christian inclusivity and community, and Christian social action and justice. We serve among those seeking and celebrating the integration of their spirituality and sexuality.

According to founder, Rev. Perry, with the statement that UFMCC seeks "integration of their spirituality and sexuality" UFMCC sets the precedent as the first Christian denomination to comply in a manner intrinsic to its structure, vision and direction.

As a denomination, UFMCC identifies as Christian in its values and beliefs. It affirms (1) a triune God who is omniscient, omnipresent and omnipotent—God, Jesus Christ, and the Holy Spirit; (2) the revelation of God through the Bible, which is the inspired Word of God; (3) belief in Jesus as fully God and having been fully man incarnate on Earth; (4) that the Holy Spirit helps people to know God's love; and (5) belief that justification comes through Jesus Christ.

In spite of its Christian values, UFMCC departs from traditional Christian values in its acceptance of same-sex behavior and LGB self-identification with the contemporary sociocultural gay movement. The first point of consideration, according to UFMCC, is to interpret and understand the Bible within its context, including characteristics of the original culture in which the Bible was written, the audience and reasons behind specific writings, as well as the identity of the authors. In the case of sexual behavior and identification, it is purported that during biblical times the cultural emphasis, different from the present, was on reproduction and multiplication. Individuals were instructed to multiply because a steady increase in population was required for survival. UFMCC approaches the interpretation of Scripture by focusing on a number of aspects (e.g., sexuality, gender, and so on) and is more consistent with approaches that are not literal interpretations or strictly adhering to the text.[7] UFMCC's second point of consideration is that the Bible's content was originally disseminated through an oral tradition and written in languages that today require translation. The original text is therefore subject to personal judgment and potential human error in interpretation. Consequently, UFMCC regards the biblical passages, which appear to condemn homosexuality, as being faulty interpretations of historical instruction. However, these views on the interpretation and authority of Scripture expressed by UFMCC have been rejected by many in traditional, conservative circles.[8]

Exodus North America

At the other end of the spectrum, we sought out participants who, despite their feelings of same-sex attraction, dis-identified with a gay, lesbian, or bisexual identity. The individuals were located through Exodus-affiliated ministries. According to the Exodus website, Exodus "is a worldwide interdenominational, Christian organization called to encourage, strengthen, unify, and equip Christians to minister the transforming power of the Lord Jesus Christ to those affected by homosexuality" (www.exodus-international.org), and the largest Christian organization that ministers to those struggling with homosexuality.[9] As a non-profit organization that espouses interdenominational Christian values, the message that Exodus seeks to promote is one of "freedom from homosexuality through the power of Jesus Christ."

History of Exodus Ministries

In the 1970s, ex-gay ministries were practically non-existent. One man, Michael Bussee, had just become a Christian, and within that year, upon feeling he had resolved his issues with homosexuality, was married. He founded a ministry which would assist others who felt distressed by their feelings of homosexual attraction. He and Jim Kaspar worked with people who were actively engaging in same-sex behavior through a ministry called "Exit Hotline," an affiliation of Melodyland Christian Center in Anaheim, CA. In September 1976, Bussee and Kaspar met with other ex-gay ministry leaders, and altogether, 40 people from different, unaffiliated ministries shared their ideas and beginnings. In addition to deciding that, collectively, these ministries would be known as "Exodus," the leaders set up annual conferences. Three years after the inception of Exodus, Bussee decided to return to same-sex behavior with Gary Cooper, a volunteer member of Exit. Bussee left his wife, daughter, and the ministry. In 1982, Bussee and Cooper held a "holy union" ceremony in a Metropolitan Community Church. And although other ministry leaders, including Ron Dennis of Theophilis Ministries, tried to change Bussee's mind, he made it clear that he had decided to actively participate in the gay community. Bussee and Cooper were, in 1990, said to have "denounced all such programs that seek to 'convert' homosexuals into heterosexuality." Bussee is also purported to have said that, "There may very well be people out there that I talked to who are dead now because they committed suicide because of the guilt that I inadvertently heaped on them." Gary Cooper died in 1993 of HIV/AIDS-related illnesses. At present, Michael Bussee is still active in the gay community.

Despite these tumultuous beginnings, Exodus is considered to be the largest Christian organization in the world to provide information and referrals to individuals who struggle with issues of homosexuality. Exodus has over 135 ministries in 17 countries, including 100 in North America.

Tenets of Exodus

As a Christian organization, Exodus seeks not only to equip individuals and agencies to communicate freedom from homosexuality[10] in an effective manner, but also to provide families and friends with understanding and support if someone they love is gay. Another goal of Exodus is to act as a bridge between those who hold extreme and incompatible views of homosexuality: those who fear it, and those who uphold it as a valid, godly way to live. In the mission statement, Exodus is "proclaiming to, educating, and impacting the world with the Biblical truth that freedom from homosexuality is possible when Jesus is Lord of one's life" (cited from www.exodus-international.org). An expanded version of this statement is found in its healing statement:

> Exodus affirms reorientation of same-sex attraction is possible. This is a process, which begins with motivation to, and self-determination to change based upon a personal relationship with Jesus Christ. We facilitate resources for this process through our member ministries, other established networks and the Church. The key outcome of this is measured by a growing capacity to turn away from temptations, a reconciling of one's identity with Jesus Christ, being transformed into His image. This enables growth towards Godly heterosexuality. Exodus recognizes that a lifelong and healthy marriage as well as a Godly single life are good indicators of this transformation.

Heterosexuality is therefore declared by Exodus to be God's created intent, whereas homosexuality (same-sex behavior and identity) falls outside God's will. Just as other sinful behaviors succumb to the power of the cross, Exodus recognizes that sexual redemption from homosexuality is available through Christ; this process of freedom is experienced as an individual gains understanding into one's own identity created in Christ and ministered by His Church.

The Exodus doctrine comprises the following: (1) Both Old and New Testament scriptures are God's inspired word useful for instruction and correction in living; (2) one God who exists in three persons—Father, Son and Holy Spirit; (3) the deity of Jesus Christ as fully man and fully God, who was conceived by the Holy Spirit, born of the virgin Mary, and sinless throughout His life. After His crucifixion, Jesus was buried and rose physically from the dead and has ascended to be with the Father; (4) only faith in Jesus Christ as one's savior can save a person from sin and the consequences of death; (5) the Holy Spirit renews individuals and enables them to grow further in their relationship with the Father; and (6) the Church is comprised of all who believe in Jesus Christ as their savior regardless of religious affiliation and denomination.

The Sexual Identity Project

The Sexual Identity Project described in this book actually consists of two separate studies. The first is a pilot study[11] in which we interviewed 14 LGB-identified individuals and 14 LGB-dis-identified individuals. Participants were selected through a concerted sampling process, in which we identified and spoke with gatekeepers in both the LGB and ex-gay communities who agreed to provide the study to potential candidates and direct them to us. Individuals from the LGB community were solicited through contact with a pastor of the UFMCC. Likewise, we spoke with a leader of an Exodus-affiliated ministry who agreed to make the study available to potential participants. Interested individuals contacted researchers directly, thus guarding their confidentiality as it pertained to gatekeepers' knowledge of participants' involvement in the study.

In the larger survey study we again sought to identify participants who espoused a Christian worldview and who either identified or dis-identified with an LGB identity. We again contacted gatekeepers from key organizations who had contact with gay and lesbian identified and dis-identified persons. Each of these individuals was asked to inquire whether members of their organizations would be willing to volunteer as participants in our research study. Participants needed to be at least 18 years of age and to have identified as LGB or dis-identified as LGB for a minimum of two years. The assumption here is that the length of time as privately and publicly identified as gay or ex-gay signifies a level of resolve or commitment to one's sexual identity, or to that which we refer in our analysis as one's sexual identity synthesis.[12]

Questionnaires were mailed to each gatekeeper for distribution, and since the survey was anonymous, gatekeepers were unaware of which member(s) in their congregation or ministry had participated, unless participants themselves informed pastors and ministry leaders. Upon return of the surveys, they were scored and qualitative data was separated from quantitative information. Qualitative data was subsequently disassembled into salient themes via content analysis by the researchers. This method is considered appropriate for analyzing relatively unexplored research questions.[13] Each researcher analyzed the qualitative data independently and shared identified themes; this process continued until consensus was reached on themes and subthemes. Quantitative data such as frequency distributions and other statistics were computed using SPSS.

The Questionnaire

The questionnaire items were a mixture of open-ended and multiple-choice questions based on existing theories and research on sexual identity development, as well as themes derived from the qualitative pilot study (pilot study interview questions and questionnaires for the second study are listed in Appendices A-C). Questionnaires were first sent to gatekeepers of both UFMCC and Exodus for review and feedback. Revised questionnaires were then made available to participants. In addition to several questions about key milestone events in personal experience of sexual identity development, we asked participants about sexual orientation, identity, and religion as influences that facilitated their reconsideration to identify or dis-identify as LGB. We also posed questions about religion and spirituality and included two instruments that measure religious commitment and intrinsic/extrinsic religiosity.

Religious Commitment Inventory—10 (RCI-10)

The RCI-10 is a 10-item Likert scaled measure of religious commitment, which is defined as "the degree to which a person adheres to his or her religious values, beliefs, and practices and employs them in daily living."[14] According to the authors, the supposition behind the RCI-10 is that an individual who is highly committed to religious values will tend to operate within the world according to the principles, beliefs, and practices inherent in a religious framework. The RCI-10 was developed according to the findings of six studies on college students, married Christian church-attending adults, undergraduates including Buddhists, Muslim, Hindu, as well as non-religious and religious clients and counselors. Means for total scores on the RCI-10 varied between 14.9 (SD = 7.1) for non-religious students, to 45.9 (SD = 4.4) for Christian counselors, with all other subgroups falling in-between. For their general sample, the mean was found to be 26 (SD = 12), and the authors concluded that scores beyond one standard deviation (i.e., a total score of 38) indicated that the individual was highly religious.

Intrinsic Religious Motivation Scale (IRMS)

The IRMS is a measure of various ways an individual expresses religiosity and the motivation one possesses for practicing religious beliefs.[15] It is a 10-item Likert scaled assessment consisting of seven items questioning intrinsic motivation, and three items measuring extrinsic motivation. Intrinsic religious motivation reflects high commitment and efforts to live their faith. In contrast, extrinsic religious motivation reflects the use of one's religion to accrue certain benefits. According to the IRMS, the lower the total score, the more intrinsically motivated the individual is, with regard to religiosity. Item scores range between 1 and 5, with the extrinsic items reverse scored. In validating the IRMS, Hoge found that the average item score was 1.97 (SD = 1.08).

Participant Demographic Information

Our study is comprised of 54 participants from across the United States. As mentioned above, the pastor of a UFMCC congregation and an Exodus ministry leader were asked to recommend gatekeepers within their ministries who they thought would assist with the current study. After confirming the participation of gatekeepers from UFMCC and Exodus, questionnaires were sent to pastors and ministry leaders, with instructions to distribute them to congregations and group members. Having anonymous questionnaires meant that gatekeepers were unaware of participants in this study unless the individuals disclosed this information to their leaders. In total, 100 questionnaires were sent to 10 UFMCC pastors for distribution. Likewise, 10 Exodus ministry leaders received 10 questionnaires each for distribution. Of the 54 participants who returned the surveys, 34 had chosen *not* to identify as gay, lesbian or bisexual, despite their experiences and feelings of same-sex attraction. These participants thus comprise the "dis-identified" sample. Conversely, 20 participants who identify with same-sex attraction and thus label themselves as LGB, comprise the "identified" sample.

In the identified sample, all 20 participants reported a Caucasian ethnicity. Twelve were male and 8 were female. Among dis-identified participants, 19 were male and 15 were female. Of the 34 dis-identified participants, 28 are Caucasian, 4 are Black, and 1 is Asian. The ages of participants in the identified sample range from 32 to 79, with a mean age of 49 years (SD = 13.38 years). Individuals in the dis-identified group range in age from 23 to 77, with a mean age of 41 years (SD = 10.65 years).

Prior to the age of 15, 23 participants in the dis-identified group, and 15 of the identified sample reported being affiliated with Protestantism. Catholicism was the religious orientation of 9 dis-identified participants and 2 identified members. Other religious affiliations include Christian Science (1 dis-identified participant), Jehovah's Witnesses (1 identified participant) and Unitarian Universalism (1 dis-identified and 1 identified participant). Two identified participants reported growing up without religious influences.

Protestantism was the predominant religious orientation for both identified and dis-identified participants, with 15 (of 20 identified) and 32 (of 34 dis-identified) individuals purporting a traditional Judeo-Christian worldview. Two dis-identified group members and no identified participants reported Catholicism as their valuative framework. Four identified participants reported "other" religious affiliations, including 1 Buddhist; one other did not identify as "Christian" per se, and two participants listed UFMCC as another religious orientation set apart from Protestant Christianity.

All participants were asked to identify their sexual orientation according to the categories "heterosexual," "homosexual," and "bisexual."

Thirty participants in the dis-identified group identified as heterosexual, whereas 2 identified as bisexual, 1 member identified as homosexual, and 1 person did not answer this question. All 20 participants in the identified group identified as homosexual.

To better understand the degree of heterosexual and homosexual orientation, as well as heterosexual and homosexual attraction each member felt, participants were asked to provide rankings from 1 (no orientation or attraction) to 10 (strong orientation or attraction) on each of these four conceptualizations. On the scale of *heterosexual orientation*, scores in the identified group ranged from 1 to 10 with a mean of 2.07 (SD = 2.34). Likewise, scores in the dis-identified group ranged from 1 to 10; however, their mean was 7.39 (SD = 2.38). On the scale of *homosexual orientation*, scores in the dis-identified group had a mean of 2.41 (SD = 1.78) with a range from 1 to 10; similarly, the identified group scores ranged from 1 to 10; however, their mean was significantly higher: 9.20 (SD = 2.14). Scores for *heterosexual attraction* were lower than those for *heterosexual orientation* in the dis-identified group, with a range from 1 to 10 with a mean of 5.97 (SD = 2.57). In the identified group, scores for the same category were slightly higher than for *heterosexual orientation*, ranging from 1 to 10 with a mean of 2.27 (SD = 2.37). The same response pattern held for the dis-identified group in their scores of *homosexual attraction*, which ranged from 1 to 10 with a mean of 4.07 (SD = 2.38), whereas the identified group's scores remained the same, ranging from 1 to 10 with a mean of 9.20 (SD = 2.14).

In an effort to understand the participants' self-perceptions of levels of spirituality and religiosity, both dis-identified and identified group members were asked to rank each on a Likert scale from 1 ("not at all") to 10 ("very"). Similar scores were obtained for both groups. Whereas the dis-identified group reported a religiosity score ranging from 2 to 9 with a mean of 7.12 (SD = 2.55), the identified group's scores ranged from 3 to 9 with a mean of 7.6 (SD = 1.96). Scores for spirituality were slightly higher in both groups, ranging from 5 to 9 in the dis-identified group (Mean = 8.21, SD = 1.11). The identified group reported the same range—5 to 9—with a mean of 8.10 (SD = 1.21).

Although these two Christian groups may seem vastly different in their worldviews, aspects of their experience are more similar across the groups, than within. For example, not all members of the dis-identified group share the exact childhood background. Not all members were sexually abused, and not all had distant relationships with their same-sex parent. By the same token, not all members of the identified group knew they were "different" at age five. There is clearly great variability of individual experience within each sample group. Our purpose for conducting these surveys was to explore common milestone events or themes in the lives of these people. How were they similar? How were they different? Do they express greater similarity or greater difference?

Chapter 4

Sexual Identity Dilemma

Introduction

The *dilemma* we refer to in *sexual identity dilemma*, is one's experience of same-sex attraction when the vast majority of peers feel predominantly or exclusively opposite-sex attraction. Consider the following example:

> A couple of years ago "Jeff," age 17, came in for therapy. In the course of time he admitted to the therapist that he suspected he was gay and wanted to consider options. Shortly following the initial discussion of his sexual orientation identity, Jeff stated that he was mistaken and that he was heterosexual. The following week he stated he thought he was gay. After some discussion, Jeff admitted that several of his friends made offensive jokes about homosexuals the previous week and that this experience probably had an impact on his sudden identity conversion. Two weeks later he was fairly sure he was heterosexual. He talked about feeling emotionally and sexually attracted to a woman at work.[1]

Jeff presents himself as a rather straightforward example of a young man who clearly has a degree of same-sex attraction, but who is also confused by these feelings (in the context of perceived peer group disapproval). He is sorting out how to navigate the key issues related to identity and identity roles most teens encounter during adolescence. Jeff experienced his attractions as a kind of dilemma in the context of his peer group.

As Jeff's story suggests, one way to understand the sexual identity dilemma is to frame it in a developmental context. Erikson[2] distinguished "identity role versus role confusion" as the key psychosocial task of adolescence. During this developmental period young people often experiment with a variety of roles in different relationships, such as with one's peer group and family, as well as within an assortment of surroundings, including school, home, and work settings. By trying on various roles, a young person can, it is believed, cultivate a sense of self and identity. In short, this amounts to a process of identity formation.

The dilemma of young people is often referred to as "sexual identity confusion" in literature pertaining to sexual identity development and synthesis.[3] The "confusion" typically arises when a person questions his or her identity after undergoing unexpected attraction to the same sex. We also refer to this time as a period of sexual identity confusion in our original pilot study. We think that the dilemma can be experienced as confusing; however, the data we gathered suggests that although most participants reported confusion, not all did. The word "dilemma" seems to address the potential complexities of an individual's *objective* circumstances (i.e., feeling same-sex attraction in a predominantly heterosexual society) without claiming that *subjective* feelings of confusion are normative for those who feel same-sex attraction and are uncertain of its significance. We therefore consider how sexual identity dilemma is recalled by those who have integrated their experiences of same-sex attraction into a lesbian, gay or bisexual (LGB) identity, and those who have dis-identified with an LGB identity.

Undoubtedly some teens do experience this dilemma. We mentioned in Chapter 1 that in a large study of over 34,000 adolescents, Remafedi and his colleagues[4] revealed that nearly 11% reported feeling "unsure" of sexual orientation and that only about 1% reported either a homosexual or bisexual orientation. What is interesting is that the best estimate of self-identification as LGB in adulthood is about 1-3% of the population, with closer to 4-6% of the population reporting feelings of attraction to members of the same sex.[5] Although it is difficult to interpret this finding with certitude, one interpretation is that many more teens may experience a sexual identity dilemma that is eventually resolved by adulthood, at least with respect to public identification (and possibly private identification as well). In other words, although the studies we cited are not longitudinal studies (so we are cautious about interpretation), many teens who experience confusion about their sexual identity may not identify as having a homosexual orientation in adulthood. Yet the dilemma is regarded as a common experience, and is cited in several models of general homosexual, gay male, and lesbian sexual identity development.

For example, Cass's[6] first stage of sexual identity development is represented by the experience of *sexual identity confusion*. The confusion seems to reflect efforts by the individual to make sense of same-sex attraction. Self-labeling is critical for Cass, as a person begins to consider first-person references to an LGB identity, something which had previously been an abstract and distant concept.

The confusion identified by Cass is noted by other theorists as well. For example, Coleman's[7] *pre-coming out* stage is a time when the person begins to view oneself as different from others. The outcome of this realization process can result in confusion, low self-esteem, or other negative feelings, including (in more extreme cases) emotional crisis. Although Troiden[8] refers to these experiences as a time of *sensitization*—in which the person feels marginalized for being different from peers—Troiden's second stage, that of *identity confusion*, occurs when the adolescent struggles with increasingly negative emotions revolving around the homosexual stigma.

Grace[9] also identifies a period when a young person feels different from his or her peers. This commonly occurs in childhood (the *emergence stage*), and these feelings can potentially lead to shame and anxiety, and other negative emotions, which often intensify during the *acknowledgement stage*, when an adolescent typically experiences same-sex attraction.

Among the models of gay male sexual identity development, Minton and McDonald[10] refer to a first stage (*symbiotic*) in which a young person recognizes that he feels different from others. Similarly, in Sophie's[11] model of lesbian identity development (*first awareness*), a young person recognizes that she is different from others and may detect a corresponding alienation from herself, or at least from identifying with feelings of same-sex attraction.

A point of contrast can be found in the Chapman and Brannock[12] model of lesbian identity development in that the theorists claim that lesbian identity precedes feelings of confusion. A young woman might later experience heightened *incongruence* (characterized by feelings of isolation and confusion) when she compares her experiences to the heterosexual norm (e.g., female desire to date males).

Although not an exhaustive review of the many theories of sexual identity development and synthesis, we can glean from these selected theories a common thread, in that most people who experience same-sex attraction also report an emotional response often characterized by confusion and incongruence. Moreover, a sense of dilemma can occur when one acknowledges that same-sex attraction or emotional connection to the same sex is outside the peer group norm and in opposition to a predominantly heterosexual society.

Before we consider our sample with respect to responses to feelings of same-sex attraction, we will examine the psychological processes in evidence during the stage of sexual identity confusion. In addition to the dilemma as a milestone event for those who experience same-sex attraction, we give credence to a number of psychological processes underway at this time, including the occurrence of confusion.

We turn now to the Sexual Identity Project. We look primarily at data gathered from the questionnaires completed by 20 LGB-identified and 34 LGB-dis-identified participants. When applicable, we also examine the pilot data gathered from interviews with 14 LGB-identified and 14 dis-identified interviewees.

The Sexual Identity Project

The first two questions in our questionnaire were intentionally broad and open-ended. We first asked respondents to describe their experiences of same-sex attraction and how they came to identify or dis-identify with an LGB identity. We then asked if they coped with same-sex attraction by connecting their experiences to the "big picture" (of God, or their vision of theirlives), which we discuss further in Chapter 6. Although we do not list all the themes emerging from the first question, we point out themes relevant to sexual identity confusion.

Tell Your Story

The experience of confusion or a sense of dilemma regarding one's sexual identity was multifaceted for those who eventually came to identify as LGB within our sample. For example, one individual's resolution was almost immediate after years of uncertainty: "I came out as a lesbian . . . when I was 16. I was clueless. It was by meeting two lesbians—and in a single instant, I made the connection. 'That's it! They're lesbians—and so am I.'" Other individuals reported different feelings, although they did not know "why" until later:

My earlier thoughts of gender were that I was "mis-assigned." I never wanted a husband and children, I wanted a wife, but had no real understanding of sexuality and attractions until my teens. I knew I was different, but didn't know how or why.

So the dilemma for some can be addressed immediately with attributions about what same-sex attraction means in light of models of LGB identification. For others, the dilemma persists and is only resolved over time.

Yet, for still others, despite acknowledging feelings of same-sex attraction, preconceptions about what their life was supposed to be—via societal values—were precipitants of confusion and hindrances to LGB identification. One individual stated,

I knew at 11. I liked boys sexually over girls. It took me 11 years of straight marriage, then two years of counseling to overcome the "catholic abhorrence" taught to me in my youth of homosexuality. A small voice— do the straight thing for your parents.

Similarly, another individual who claimed that his sexual identity was determined at (or prior to) birth, reported the following:

I was born gay, although I did not really know it. When I was a child, I always assumed the "female" role when I played pretend. I am a 42-year-old male, was married to a woman for eight years and have two children.

Another factor contributing to the sense of dilemma has been silence and isolation, which precluded identification for one woman:

As long as I can remember, I have been attracted to women. Not until after high school did I identify my same-sex attraction and label as being a "lesbian." I noticed in high school other girls interacting "differently" with each other, but didn't know how to go about approaching the subject. I was, you might say, a quiet one. Never questioned or acted on my feelings until I was approached at the age of 21.

For some in the identified sample, confusion or a sense of dilemma when considering sexual identity was never an issue in retrospect. One individual stated, "I realized at an early age that I was attracted to the same sex. I have had several same-sex experiences and definitely consider myself gay. I believe I was born that way and it was not a mere choice." As with the LGB-identified participants, the experience of sexual identity dilemma was not singular for the individuals who eventually dis-identified with an LGB identity. Although the experience of same-sex attraction was noticed early in their lives, the ways in which the feelings, behavior or thoughts unfolded—or did not unfold—varied considerably. For some dis-identified individuals, the feelings of difference alerted them that something set them apart from others:

> I always felt like I was an anomaly among my peers growing up. I realized there was some fascination with the same sex as my body matured, but it wasn't until a friend "seduced" me in college that I realized it was more than just curiosity.

For other individuals, sexual identity was called into question with the experience of confusion, which was certainly a reality:

> I began to notice that I was attracted to the same sex around the age of nine. Although having those feelings, I also liked girls and liked the idea of having a girlfriend. I had a sexual experience with another male and later began to act out on other male children my age (oral, touching private parts). When I reached adolescence, my attraction became more sexual and I always was curious of what other guys looked like and what it would feel like to touch them. I struggled secretly for years and wondered if I was really gay. I did not want to act on my secret feelings, but could not understand why my feelings were so strong and why they would not just go away.

The dilemma manifest itself as confusion, which may have been exacerbated by the acknowledged same-sex attraction, both in contrast to the heterosexual norm and in isolation and secrecy from others.

Another individual reported that his feelings of same-sex attraction were largely due to a gender crisis rather than confusion regarding his sexual identity:

> At a young age, I was or became aware that I was viewing other men differently and didn't identify with them as well as I did with the girls. Basically, I had a gender crisis. After seeking residential help, I found out more about what was underneath the same-sex issue. A desire to be a man, but not knowing how to be a man.

The relationship between gender identity confusion and sexual identity dilemma is not well understood. There is apparently a link between the two, as about 75% of which are accurately diagnosed with Gender Identity Disorder in childhood will have a homosexual or bisexual orientation in adulthood (Diagnostic and Statistical Manual of Mental Disorders-Fourth Edition, 1994). Yet gender identity is only one of many facets of the broader construct of sexual identity, and the relationship between the constructs needs further exploration.

Although some dis-identified individuals in the sample detected same-sex attraction, it tended to be recalled as an emotional longing prior to becoming a physical or sexual desire. One individual stated,

> I was a "tomboy." In the 8th grade I was attracted to the girls' star basketball player. Nothing of a sexual nature occurred. I felt a few other girl attractions, but never acted on any until I fell in love with a friend after I was married.

Yet, for others, it was the converse: the attraction was predominantly physical rather than emotional as such. Consider the following example:

> I never wanted to date men, which is common in the homosexual community, but I frequently masturbated thinking about being with a man sexually. I have never identified myself as gay, but I wondered a lot since I had these fantasies.

The experience of sexual identity dilemma can therefore become apparent as an objective reality, although the subjective experience of confusion may or may not be reported. Among those who identify and those who dis-identify, the dilemma itself can be experienced in diverse ways.

Experiences of Same-Sex Attraction

Following the open-ended question about individual stories, we asked specific questions about experience of same-sex attraction. Specifically, we asked at what age participants recalled first noticing feelings of same-sex attraction. We also asked whether respondents felt confused or tense about feeling what would later be identified as same-sex attraction.

The age at which respondents first remembered to have had feelings of same-sex attraction were as follow: Each participant who identified with an LGB identity completed this item; the mean ages at time of recollection were 9.6 years (SD = 3.0 years) for males and 14 years of age (SD = 8.6 years) for females. Thirty-three out of 34 of the dis-identified respondents answered this question. The mean ages at time of recollection among respondents were 10.5 years of age (SD = 4.6 years) for males and 14.3 years (SD = 4.1 years) for females. Apparently, both groups first noted same-sex attraction at approximately the same age, without obvious differences between the LGB-identified and dis-identified groups. Statistical analysis reveals a significant distinction for the factor of gender, not LGB-identification. On average, males first noticed these feelings at age 10.2 (range = 3-25, SD = 3.98), whereas females became aware of same-sex attraction at age 14.2 (range = 5-28, SD = 5.89) ($F(1, 51) = 8.90$, $p = .004$). Thus, females were more likely to become aware of these attractions at a later age compared with males.

Feeling Different for Gender-Related Reasons

We also asked if respondents felt different from others growing up for gender-related reasons. The rationale behind this question is Darryl Bem's theory of the etiology of same-sex attraction. Bem holds that our society enforces rather strict gender roles and that we are raised such that we come to eroticize the gender unfamiliar to us. The key appears to be whether people feel different for gender-related reasons.

In our original pilot study 11 of the 14 LGB identified interviewees reported feeling different from other children for gender-related reasons, that is, because of their choices of activities, clothing or preferred playmates. The other 3 identified participants stated that they did not feel their behavior to be any different than their peers. In the dis-identified group, 12 of 14 participants also indicated feeling different from other children for similar reasons as those offered by the identified participants. One dis-identified participant, who expressed that she did not feel different for gender-related reasons summed up her experience, "No. I was 'Becky homey-makey' . . . loved to cook and sew. . . . Loved dolls, Barbies, playing house, playing school. Not until girls fell for teen idols did I feel a difference." The other individual who reported not feeling different from her peers said that although she was a "total tomboy," she was unaware of any differences. In her experience, she was "just having a good time."

In our larger study, 15 of 20 (75%) of participants who identified with an LGB identity reported feeling different from others growing up for gender-related reasons (see Table 1). Similarly, among those who dis-identified with an LGB identity, 26 of 34 (76%) participants reported feeling different from their peers growing up for gender related reasons.

Table 1. *Did You Feel Different From Your Peers Growing Up For Gender-Related Reasons?*

	LGB-Identified	Dis-Identified
Yes	75%	76%
No	25%	24%

We asked respondents for the reasons behind the difference from others for gender-related reasons. In other words, although the majority reported feeling different from others for gender-related reasons, we wanted to pinpoint specific reasons why they felt different. When asked to identify such reasons, respondents chose from a number of options derived from the content analysis of the original pilot study. Themes of that analysis included, "My play activities as a child," "My playmates," "Things other people said to me about my behavior," "Feelings I had about myself," "Feelings I had about others," and "Feelings I had about my parents." Respondents could, if they chose, also provide other reasons.

Among the 15 respondents from the identified group who felt different for gender-related reasons, the most prominent themes were "My play activities as a child" (80.0% of respondents) and "My playmates" (73.3%). Other themes in descending order of prominence included, "Things other people said to me about my behavior" (53.3%) and "Feelings I had about others" (53.3%), "Feelings I had about myself" (46.7%), and "Feelings I had about my parents" (13.3%) (see Table 2). Thirty-five percent of respondents shared other reasons for feeling different; the themes emergent from our qualitative analysis included, "Relationships with the opposite sex" and "Preferred activities of the opposite sex," as well as "Disdain for stereotypical activities." For example, one male participant stated that he "preferred cooking, housework to sports, and summers spent with my aunts and grandmother." Another male reported, "Dad was a jock and I always hated sports."

Table 2. *Reasons for Feeling Different from One's Peers*

	Identified	Dis-Identified
"My play activities as a child."	80.0%	85.6%
"My playmates as a child."	73.3%	46.2%
"Things other people said to me about my behavior or way of relating."	53.3%	57.6%
"Feelings I had about myself."	46.7%	92.3%
"Feelings I had about others."	53.5%	61.5%
"Feelings I had about my parents."	13.3%	38.5%
Other	35.0%	30.7%

In contrast, 26 dis-identified respondents reported feeling different from others for gender-related reasons. The most prominent theme reported by them was, "Feelings I had about myself" (92.3%), followed by "My play activities as a child" (85.6%). Other reasons for feeling different included, "Feelings I had about others" (61.5%), "Things other people said to me about my behavior" (57.6%), "My playmates" (46.2%), and "Feelings I had about my parents" (38.5%). About 31% of respondents shared additional reasons for feeling different from others, and the themes emergent from the qualitative analysis included, "Sexual experiences," "Sexual molestation," "Wanted to be other sex," and "Someone said the person was 'different.'" For instance, one male participant reported that he was "introduced to homosexual sex by an older male friend." One female stated that her sense of being "different" was attributed by family, "My mother told me I was 'different' from her other children when I was a baby with two sisters and one brother."

These responses highlight the fact that the majority of both LGB-identified and dis-identified participants in our study felt different from their peers for gender-related reasons. The specifics of that experience showed considerable within-group and between-group variance.

Experiences of Confusion or Tension

We also asked if respondents felt confusion or tension about having experiences of same-sex attraction. In our original pilot study, 8 of 14 LGB identified participants reported feeling confused regarding their same-sex attraction for various reasons, such as physical attraction towards members of the same-sex, not being attracted to members of the opposite sex, or confusion because they could not find a niche. Two of the 6 identified participants did not experience confusion because they lacked a vocabulary for same-sex attraction: "I didn't talk about it in childhood. There was no terminology for it." One respondent summed up her experience of not being confused by stating, "I was never confused. I was confident I was straight until I was confident I was gay."

Of the individuals who were dis-identified from the pilot interviews, 12 of 14 reported feelings of confusion that may have been due to negative emotions (e.g., shame and denial), a lack of understanding of behaviors (e.g., "I couldn't figure out the kissing thing. I never let boys kiss me.") and the reaction of others. Reasons cited by the other 2 respondents for not feeling confused include being unaware and lacking understanding.

In the current study we asked whether each person recalled feeling tense about same-sex attraction. Twenty-eight of 34 (82%) dis-identified participants confirmed this experience. Again, a similar percentage of the identified participants remembered a similar tension, as 16 of 20 (80%) stated that they felt these feelings.

The subjective experiences of tension and confusion are common among both those who identify and those who dis-identify with an LGB-identity synthesis. We examine in Chapter 5 how people respond to this objective dilemma and to these subjective feelings; we also scrutinize a variety of themes as we explore how sexual identity develops over time, and at the role of attributions and meaning-making during sexual identity development and (eventually) synthesis. But first we turn to a discussion of themes and psychological processes evident during the stage of *identity dilemma*.

Themes and Psychological Processes

Which themes and psychological processes can be identified from the information provided by participants in our study? We begin by agreeing with Diamond,[13] who confirms the assumption by many in the field, that sexual orientation identity is "a stable trait that exerts a monotonic press on behavior, ideation, or attraction (or all three) at an early age and is fully formed by adolescence." Diamond points out that the later development of sexual orientation identity among women is due to "underlying properties of female psychosexual development," a cohort effect (that reflects more on sociocultural factors), or "restrictive cultural environments."[14] We will discuss the implications of Diamond's observations in Chapters 6 and 7, but we wonder whether the gap between initial attractions and full identity synthesis may partly be due to conflict between explanatory frameworks: traditional Christian and LGB-affirming ideologies. For Wolkomir,[15] the conflict itself requires that, to some extent, both LGB-identifying and LGB-dis-identifying individuals revise early childhood theological assumptions; they proceed to develop an alternative hermeneutical approach to validate their life trajectory in order to correspond with personal experience. We address these issues in greater detail in later chapters.

As we begin to recognize the "dilemma" in sexual identity dilemma, we might consider how alternatives to an LGB identity are treated in the literature. For example, we note that Cass[16] believed that "acceptance" of experiences of same-sex attraction (resulting in LGB identification) is one possible outcome, while others include "foreclosure," which may be interpreted as a rejection of one's "true identity" (due to the meaning of unwanted attractions, or because attributions about the meaning of same-sex attractions are incorrect).

For Troiden,[17] potential themes and psychological processes included acceptance, denial, minimization, and various related coping skills. Acceptance is seen as coming to terms with same-sex attraction thus signaling who a person "really is." In contrast, denial and minimization are two ways people rebuke acceptance by ignoring or discounting the idea that same-sex attraction is indicative of the essential person. Coping— and, in particular, problem-focused coping—is used to reduce, diminish or eradicate homoerotic feelings, including avoidance of same-sex behaviors, which Troiden views as unhealthy. Troiden acknowledges that other attributions can be operative and that these attributions are typically more appealing to the person, such as "This is just a temporary identity."

In keeping with the theme of avoidant behavior, Grace[18] believed that, during the *acknowledgement* stage, some individuals may foreclose on an LGB identity because of internalized homophobia. Thus, foreclosure is again highlighted as a psychological process commonly experienced alongside experiences of confusion or tension.

In contrast, Chapman and Brannock's[19] model of lesbian identity development holds that lesbian identity precedes feelings of confusion. An initial and apparently critical experience in this model is that of incongruency between a young woman's experiences and those of others. The move toward labeling oneself as "lesbian" occurs out of the context of any number of experiences with others. The specific psychological processes are unclear, but they appear to relate to incongruency and feelings of isolation and separation from non-lesbian others.

The key psychological process in McCarn and Fassinger's[20] model of lesbian identity is awareness. That is, the young woman becomes increasingly aware that her experience differs from the norm. Awareness occurs with reference to "individual sexual identity" and "group membership identity," meaning that the young woman makes the self-defining attribution, "I am lesbian," and affiliates with the broader LGB community and those who share this explanatory framework.

Some of these themes and psychological processes may be best understood as we consider the role of attributions and meaning making, a focus of the next chapter. A young person's feeling of same sex attraction may often coincide with a dilemma, which is often felt as confusion or tension. What will become clearer in the context of sexual identity development is how a person makes connections between present circumstances, including coping resources, and a broader worldview.

As we consider the results from our study, we hesitate to describe responses to the dilemma of experiencing same-sex attraction in a predominantly heterosexual society by pathologizing any one response. We avoid the characterizations of various coping responses as either "foreclosure" on an LGB identity or as evidence of internalized homophobia. However, this should not be understood as our rejection of the homophobia construct but merely a rejection of the *a priori* assumption that all efforts to dis-identify with an LGB identity are manifestations of internalized homophobia.[21]

Figure 1. *Themes Characteristic of Sexual Identity Dilemma*

Experiences of SSA	Felt different for gender-related reasons?	Confusion?
~ 10 yrs. (Males) ~ 14 yrs. (Females)	75% LGB-Id 76% LGB-Dis-Id Prominent themes: - "Play activities" (LGB-Id/Dis-Id) - "Playmates" (LGB-Id) - "Feelings I had about myself" (LGB Dis-Id)	80% LGB-Id 82% LGB Dis-Id

In refusing to pathologize any one response during sexual identity dilemma, we remind the reader that this is not the focus of the present study. Rather, we report on two broad and divergent trajectories that transport sexual identity development through to sexual identity synthesis. These trajectories appear to begin to diverge with attributions and meaning making, which we shall clarify in the following chapter. Even at the point of dilemma, however, both groups report a wide range of experiences.

That males and females from both the LGB identified and dis-identified groups reported differences in age of first experiences of same-sex attraction is certainly noteworthy. Males tended to recall same-sex attraction at a younger age, typically around age 10. Females, in contrast, recalled same-sex attraction on average at around age 14. These differences are true, regardless of where a person ends up in their self-report of sexual identity synthesis later in life.

The majority of both LGB identified and LGB dis-identified participants also reported feeling different for gender related reasons. Both groups primarily highlighted play activities as a significant factor in their feeling different. Groups tended to differ in other experiences, such as playmates, which a higher percentage of LGB identified individuals noted, and feelings about oneself, which the LGB-dis-identified individuals were more likely to note. Moreover, about the same percentage of both groups did not report feeling different from their peers for gender-related reasons.

The two groups were also very similar in their memory of feeling confused by same-sex attraction. Again, as with feeling different for gender-related reasons, about the same percentage of individuals in both groups did not report feeling confused in response to their experience of same-sex attraction.

In addition to these findings, what strikes us are the challenges both groups face in responding to their dilemma. If we return to the initial construct of sexual identity, we notice the multifaceted aspects of the identity itself: prevalence and direction of sexual attractions, gender identity, biological sex, beliefs and values about sexual behavior, and so on. These aspects of sexual identity may be weighted differently for different people at different times in their lives, and the between-group differences may become more evident as we examine how sexual identity develops and synthesizes over time. At present, however, there appear to be more similarities than differences between the two groups.

We are beginning to see that during identity dilemma, both LGB-identified and LGB-dis-identified respondents report that the persistence and direction of sexual attraction is rather prominent. The persistence and direction of attraction may be reported by some, although others report a vague sense of feeling "different" from others, and for a fairly high percentage, feeling "different" is associated with gender-related reasons. Upon reflection, these experiences may be understood as same-sex attraction. In any case, these experiences contrast rather sharply with the heterosexual norm and begin to shape the contours of the dilemma. We heard some respondents mention gender identity confusion and raise questions, referring perhaps to their biological sex, but this was far less frequent; gender identity confusion may factor in as less relative to the persistence and direction of sexual attraction. Similarly, volition/intention and one's beliefs and values may play a role during sexual identity dilemma but they are less pronounced. In other words, one does not *choose* to experience same-sex attraction; rather, the individual merely feels same-sex attraction. We examine in the next two chapters whether experiences shared by those who identify and those who dis-identify with an LGB identity lead to different weighted experiences of these aspects of sexual identity.

Chapter 5

Sexual Identity Development

Introduction

The preceding chapter offered insights into the dilemma encountered by individuals when they experience same-sex attraction. The fact that they have homoerotic attractions in a predominantly heterosexual society represents the dilemma. As the individual begins to construct meaning out of experience, it can lead him or her into a variety of emotions and psychological processes, possible confusion, and in some cases, crisis, as well as a shift in initial attributions.

These themes are developed further here, as we turn to the ways in which our two groups—those who *identify* with their feelings of same-sex attraction and integrate experience into a lesbian, gay or bisexual (LGB) identity synthesis and those who *dis-identify* with an LGB identity—develop their sexual identity against the backdrop of this dilemma. To use an analogy, if the dilemma is the foundation, how do these two groups build a sexual identity upon such a tumultuous basis?

The aforementioned descriptions of models of sexual identity development do not assert a clear connection with either essentialism or social constructionism. For example, several models use language suggesting that sexual identity "development" is merely active acknowledgment of an existing identity. However, sexual identity development resembles more an unveiling of an existing identity—as it presents to self and others one's authenticity as a person. We mentioned the metaphysical debate on sexual orientation in Chapter 1, that the two contrasting viewpoints, essentialism and constructionism, hold different assumptions about the nature of sexual orientation. The unveiling of who one "truly is" rings stronger of essentialism, where not only are the categories of hetero-sexual, homosexual, and bisexual "natural human kinds,"[1] but that they are also fundamental aspects of self-hood. To fail to uncover one's true identity is to deny what properly defines the core of a person.

Essentialist assumptions and descriptions, while implicit in a number of models of sexual identity development, are rejected by other theorists who favor a social constructionist model[2] in which "people translate the everyday understanding of lesbian, gay, or bisexual identity provided by the Western indigenous psychologies into knowledge, behaviors, beliefs, and experiences about themselves via the process of reciprocal interaction."[3] The *development* in sexual identity development refers to the key milestone events that bring together social, emotional and sexual dimensions for connecting with others.

Whether essentialist or constructionist, we can nevertheless examine how the broader construct of sexual identity develops over time. Although we might look for language that confirms either essentialist or constructionist assumptions, the actual terms used to understand the experience of sexual identity development can come from theorists or researchers or from those they study.

Milestone Events and Psychological Processes

As we begin to consider sexual identity development, it may be helpful to distinguish between the milestone events and psychological processes believed to characterize different stages or phases of identity formation. The general consensus is that the sequence of milestone events is as follows: (1) experience of same-sex attraction, (2) engagement in same-sex behavior, (3) labeling oneself as homosexual, (4) disclosure of an LGB identity to others, and (5) relationship with another member of the same sex. Other researchers[4] have also reported that same-sex behavior precedes labelling, particularly among males who later self-identify as gay. As Dube and Savin-Williams[5] suggest, the timing of the milestone events may vary somewhat by gender and ethnicity. For example, in their study of White, Black, Asian, and Latino adolescents, milestone events were reported at specific age ranges that were generally consistent (see Table 1) for ethnic minority adolescents, with the exception of Asian young adults, who were more likely to label themselves as homosexual prior to engaging in same-sex behavior. Similarly, in Diamond's study[6] many of the 89 self-identifying lesbian or bisexual young women fit into average age ranges for milestone events. However, a large proportion does not fit neatly into at least one milestone event; this observation suggests greater heterogeneity of experience than what is often presumed. In any case, results of studies in this area indicate key milestone events and a general developmental pathway, which might then be understood with reference to various psychological processes, such as attributions and meaning-making.

Table 1. *Average Age Range in Years at Time of Milestone Events*

Awareness	SSB	Label	Disclosure	Relationship
8-11	12-15	15-18	17-19	18-20

Note: Awareness = first awareness of feelings of same-sex attraction; SSB = same-sex behavior; Label = first labeling of oneself as gay, lesbian or bisexual; Disclosure = first disclosure to another person; Relationship = first relationship with the same sex.

These milestone events, therefore, give us insight into how specific experiences shape identity. But they impart little about the psychological processes accompanying the milestone events themselves. How does a person construct meaning from a specific milestone event, such as same-sex behavior? What leads one person to label themselves as "gay" or "lesbian" while another does not? Are there psychological processes that distinguish between those who do—and those who do not—make a self-defining attribution that same-sex attraction or behavior signals who the person 'really is'?

Early theorists discussed some of these psychological processes, but often from the perspective that an LGB identity synthesis[7] is a normative outcome. For example, Cass[8] discusses the transition from tolerating an LGB identity (*Identity Tolerance*) to having a sense of peace (*Identity Acceptance*), and eventually a feeling of pride (*Identity Pride*) in that identity. The attribution implicit in the Cass model is that same-sex attraction suggests that the person is LGB. There is a progression from probably being LGB—to acceptance of that identity—to pride in that identity. The pathway is streamlined by involvement with others who share similar perspectives about an LGB identity. There is also a shift from extremist thinking (for example, "homosexuals are good, heterosexuals are oppressive") to a more subtle appreciation of the positive and negative aspects of both the gay and the heterosexual community. Doing so represents a transition from incongruence to congruence in terms of attributions and meaning-making.

Coleman[9] discusses a similar process. A person acknowledges an emerging LGB identity and makes selective disclosures (*Coming-out*), followed by involvement with others who make similar attributions about same-sex attraction (*Explanation*). This leads to *First Relationship*, or the search for sexual and emotional connection and intimacy with others. The acknowledgement appears to be critical to the potential consideration of an LGB identity. One must make attributions about one's experiences of same-sex attraction and construct meaning from these attributions by tying their specific experiences of same-sex attraction to a more comprehensive meaning (an LGB identity).[10]

We turn next to the experiences of those who identify and dis-identify with an LGB identity. At the end of the chapter we discuss the psychological processes engaged in during sexual identity development.

The Sexual Identity Project

Reactions to Same-Sex Attraction

In our original pilot study we asked interviewees how they dealt with their experiences of confusion or tension. Both groups were asked what initiated the questioning of their sexual identities. For 5 of the 14 LGB identified interviewees, same-sex attraction led them to begin probing into the assumption that they resembled the majority of individuals. Three participants reported that dating experiences were the springboard to questioning their sexual identity. As 1 female participant stated, "I didn't want to be gay, but nothing ever came out of dating men in college." Four LGB identified respondents expressed that they fell in love persons who happened to be of the same sex and had ongoing relationships. Five others reported not experiencing any questioning about sexual identity, although one participant did try to change his sexual focus of interest: "I don't ever remember questioning it. Even though I thought I could turn it around, I always knew. I was always attracted to men."

For the LGB-dis-identified interviewees, several different themes were salient from the responses. Nine of 14 dis-identified participants began questioning their sexual identities as soon as they felt same-sex physical and emotional attraction. For some, questioning occurred within a fantasy life. As 1 respondent puts it: "I would fantasize about men and thoughts about sexuality brought about these images." Five of 14 individuals stated that past experience of sexual abuse led them to explore their sexual identities. One respondent stated, "Being molested by a male and somewhat sexualizing it. Thinking to myself although I don't like this, I do like this. Seeing the naked male body, the closeness, etc. . . . ."

Gender-related reasons, such as associating oneself with activities generally attributed to the opposite sex, were cited by 4 of the LGB-dis-identified participants. For 3 of these same individuals, public reaction—possibly due to their non-stereotypical behaviors—led them to inquire whether they were different. Lastly, 3 dis-identified individuals cited misperceptions about oneself due to family disruptions or difficult relationships as reasons for questioning one's sexual identity. "I never connected with a strong role model. . . . I felt as though I was different, unable to connect. Therefore, I must be different."

Our experience interviewing LGB-identified and LGB-dis-identified individuals in our pilot study indicates myriad reactions to experiences of same-sex attraction. We examined the pilot responses and identified several themes, which we made available to participants in the larger survey. For example, when asked how participants in the present study tried to make meaning of the tension or confusion they reported, respondents could choose from options derived from the content analysis of the original pilot study. Themes drawn from the pilot analysis include, "I am a different sex," "Something is wrong with me," "I am damaged," "These feelings signify who I really am," "This is just a passing phase," "It really is okay to feel this way," and "I am looking for a replacement parent."

In the larger study, those who integrated their experience of same-sex attraction into an LGB identity synthesis tended to have a range of reactions. Eight of the 20 respondents (40%) thought something was wrong with them. This theme may also encompass feeling "broken" or in need of "fixing," and 20% (4 of 20) of respondents thought they were "damaged." To experience some gender confusion was not uncommon, as 30% (6 of 20) thought they were a "different sex." More LGB affirming responses, such as, "These feelings signify who I really am" and "It really is okay to feel this way" were endorsed by fewer respondents (10%), although one-fourth of respondents indicated another option altogether. The analyzed responses included the themes, "Fear of expressing feelings," "Frustration with feelings and lack of expression," and "Minimization" (e.g., saying to oneself, "I'll get over it."). So we observe among this sample a range of reactions from the start of exploration of same-sex attraction to the acceptance of identification with an LGB identity.

Dis-identified respondents answered the same question about constructing meaning from the tension/confusion they experienced at feeling same-sex attraction. The greatest percentage thought that something was "wrong" with them (n = 20 of 34, 58.8%). Interestingly, 12 respondents (35.2%) made meaning by attributing their confusion or tension to "a passing phase" (compared to only 1 respondent from the LGB identified group). Other endorsed items included, "I am a different sex" (23.5%), "I am damaged" (20.5%), "These feelings signify who I really am" (8.8%), "It really is okay to feel this way" (5.8%), and "I am looking for a replacement parent" (5.8%). As with the LGB identified group, nearly a quarter of respondents (23.5%) described another altogether different response. Responses were analyzed and included themes, "Denial of gender," "Being a 'sensitive' child," and "Sexual experimentation."

Again, similar to those who identified with an LGB identity, a variety of responses were given by those who dis-identified with an LGB identity. A significant percentage from both groups thought that something was "wrong" with them; however, it is noteworthy that given the diversity of response, no particular answer to experiences of same-sex attraction emerges to distinguish the groups. Moreover, people have a number of different responses as they first begin to construe their experiences. Thus, they appear more similar than dissimilar upon examination of the variability of significant responses.

Table 2. *Percentage of Respondents' Responses to the Statement, "I Tried to Make Meaning of the Tension/Confusion by Saying to Myself"*

	Identified	Dis-Identified
"I am a different sex."	30.0%	23.5%
"Something is wrong with me."	40.0%	58.8%
"I am damaged."	20.0%	20.5%
"These attractions signify who I really am."	10.0%	8.8%
"This is just a passing phase."	5.0%	35.2%
"It really is okay for me to feel this way."	10.0%	5.8%
"I am looking for a replacement parent."	5.0%	5.8%
Other	25.0%	23.5%

To consider how the two groups recalled reacting to experiences of same-sex attraction is certainly important because these early reactions may represent the foundation for a specific individual's attributions about the meaning of same-sex attraction. We turn now to how participants described their first awareness of a connection between themselves and the concept of "homosexuality."

Awareness of Connection to "Homosexuality"

Respondents were asked what happened to instigate their awareness of a possible connection between themselves and homosexuality. This question was adapted from an earlier study in which it was suggested that this awareness is an important milestone event among those who later self-identify as gay. As with the previous questions, the major themes were derived from our pilot study; once again respondents were given the opportunity to share additional background if their response was not captured in the commonly reported experiences. Among those who identified as LGB, the highest percentage (65%) noticed that their feelings about the same sex were different from other people's feelings; as they made comparisons, they observed that others were generally not expressing the same sentiments toward the same sex. The next most common experience was, "Feeling like I was different from people" (45%), meaning thinking to be "a different kind of person." This statement was followed by, "Other people made fun of me because I was different" (35%) and

"Others told me that I was different from other people because of the way I acted" (25%). Thirty-five percent of respondents offered a specific alternative response to the items offered, and these responses were also analyzed with the following prominent themes: "Physical experiences" (later connections made following physical experiences), "No sexual interest" (in the opposite sex), and "Read confirming literature" (regarding an LGB identity).

Table 3. *Percentage of Respondents' Answers to the Question, "What Happened to Cause That Awareness [That There Might Be a Connection Between Homosexuality and Yourself]?*

	Identified	Dis-Identified
"I felt like I was different from other people."	45.0%	29.4%
"I noticed that my feelings about members of the same sex were different from other people."	65.0%	64.7%
"Others told me that I was different from other people because of the way I acted."	25.0%	29.4%
"Other people made fun of me because I was different."	35.0%	29.4%
Other	35.0%	38.2%

Dis-identified respondents exhibited a similar response pattern (regarding the most prominent theme) to this particular item, with 22 of 34 (64.7%) reporting that feelings about the same sex differed from others' experience. The next most common experiences reported by LGB-dis-identified individuals were, "I felt like I was different from people," "Others told me that I was different from other people because of the way I acted," and "Other people made fun of me because I was different." Each of these responses were reported by a little under one-third

(29.4%) of respondents. Thirteen LGB-dis-identified individuals offered alternative responses, which were analyzed; themes identified as particularly salient include: "Same-sex sexual experiences," "Labeling by others" (another person labeled the participant), "Difficulty with sexual response when with the opposite sex," and "Counselor's encouragement to explore."

Feeling different from others and making attributions that same-sex feelings partly define some of that difference was a common reply. Feeling "different" can also be reinforced by others, presumably parents, siblings, or peer group, but we did not ask respondents for specifics. Parents, siblings, and one's peer group can also go beyond remarking merely that the individual seems "different" to them; various and more extreme reactions can include teasing or taunting someone due to these perceived or real differences.

Respondents also reported other feelings associated with awareness that they might be in the realm of "homosexuality." LGB-identified individuals reported a number of negative emotions, including "Confused" (55%), "Lonely" (35%), "Scared" (30%), "Sad" (15%), and "Angry" (5%). Twenty percent reported feeling happiness. Forty percent of the LGB-identified respondents offered alternative responses about their awareness of a possible connection to "homosexuality." Responses were analyzed and the following themes emerged: "Isolation/separation," "Shame," "Relief" (after admission), "Guilt," "Excitement," and "Peace."

The dis-identified respondents reported a similar range of negative reactions, with "Confused" and "Scared" rated as the highest percentages (64.7% and 61.7%, respectively). "Lonely" (41.1%), "Sad" (32.3%), and "Angry" (17.6%) were also reported. Two respondents (5.8%) reported feeling "Happy." Nineteen respondents (55.8%) offered alternative responses about their awareness of a possible connection to "homosexuality." Responses were analyzed and the following themes arose: "Frustration," "Relief" (associated with a sense of belonging), "Hopelessness," and "Longing for intimacy."

That a higher proportion of dis-identified respondents reported experiencing negative emotions regarding their potential association with homosexuality when compared with those who are LGB-identified is noteworthy. What is the significance of this difference? And how does it affect the current identification of these respondents?

As we move away from one's awareness of a connection between self and the concept of homosexuality, and the concomitant feelings associated with that perceived connection, we turn to initial attributions. These attributions are developed regarding a potential LGB identity and one's response to that initial attribution. We also asked whether people ever had reasons for thinking, "I'm not really LGB," or if they ever made another attribution early in their sexual identity development in order to rationalize feelings of same-sex attraction.

Initial Attributions

When asked, "Did you initially think that same-sex attraction meant you were gay or lesbian?," 13 of 20 (65%) LGB-identified individuals indicated "yes," while only 13 of 34 (38.2%) dis-identified individuals indicated "yes" to this question. The follow-up to this item asked if they did *not* think same-sex attraction meant they were gay, what did the attraction suggest (what meaning was attached to those experiences). Six of the LGB-identified and 16 of the LGB-dis-identified individuals indicated that they "really wanted to be friends with the person" they were attracted to. Two of the LGB-identified individuals and 13 of the LGB-dis-identified individuals remarked that their feelings were attributed to wanting "someone to love" them, and 2 of the LGB-identified and 5 of the LGB-dis-identified individuals indicated that their feelings were attributed to "feeling lonely" at that time. None of the LGB-identified respondents felt "sick" or "mentally ill," while 3 of the LGB-dis-identified individuals reported this attribution. Five of the LGB-identified individuals and 6 of the LGB-dis-identified individuals reported an additional response to this item. Responses were analyzed and the following themes emerged for LGB-identified participants: "Desire to explore sexuality," "Lack of models or terms like 'gay,'" and "Jealousy." Themes recorded for dis-identified participants included, "Satan attacking me," "Means of satisfying sexual urges," and "Sensitivity" (being more sensitive and emotional than other males).

Among those who initially thought same-sex attraction meant that they were gay or lesbian, some LGB-identified participants started questioning their sexual identity because: "I had same-sex attractions" (84.6% of LGB-identified), "Fantasies about same-sex individuals" (76.9%), "No matter what I tried I couldn't change the feelings of same-sex attraction" (61.5%), "Dating people of the opposite sex didn't make me feel the same way as others" (61.5%), "Other people's reactions to me" (30.7%), and "Other people's reactions to me suggested same-sex attractions (for example, comments from peers or family members)" (23%).

LGB-identified respondents were asked how they reacted upon first thinking they were LGB. The two most frequently confirmed items were, "Sought out other gay or lesbian individuals," and "Sought out same-sex sexual experiences." Another item that seemed supportive of an LGB identity also endorsed by a substantial percentage of respondents was, "Sought out information in gay or lesbian literature" (45%). Initial responses that were interventions of sorts, included, "Prayed for God to cure me," which was endorsed by 30% of respondents, and "Sought out sexual experiences with members of the opposite sex, which was purported by 20% of respondents. Many LGB-identified respondents identified items that might be viewed as "middle of the road," including, "Sought out objective information on homosexuality" (25%) and "Sought out counseling to sort through the confusion" (20%). Twenty percent of respondents reported denying their feelings because of concomitant feelings of shame. The least often reported responses were, "Avoided any appearances of homosexuality" (10%), "Avoided any thoughts or feelings related to feelings of same-sex attraction (5%), "Sought out counseling to change my sexual orientation" (5%), and "Talked to my parents" (5%). Four respondents offered other responses to this item, including, "Hid (behind other identity)," "Came out completely," "Became part of gay underground," and "Couldn't find other LGB people."

In contrast, LGB-dis-identified individuals, while validating many of the same items, did so less frequently. For example, 29.4% of the dis-identified respondents endorsed the item, "Sought out other gay or lesbian individuals," and 26.4% of the dis-identified respondents endorsed the item, "Sought out same-sex sexual experiences." Some rejected their experiences by praying for God to cure them (17.6%), or by denying their same-sex attraction due to shame (14.7%), whereas others broached the topic cautiously by seeking either objective information on homosexuality (11.7%) or information in gay and lesbian literature (11.7%). A much smaller percentage (8% compared to 20% of the LGB-identified respondents) sought counseling to sort through the confusion, and only one respondent reported seeking counseling to change sexual orientation. None of the LGB-dis-identified respondents reported engaging in sexual experiences with the opposite sex, and only 8.8% of respondents reported talking to their parents. Four respondents offered an additional response to this item and these responses were analyzed for themes. These included, "Entered into LGB relationships," "Engaged in thoughts, feelings, and fantasies," "Denial—did not label," and "Curious—explored LGB relationships."

We asked, "Before initially identifying/dis-identifying as LGB, did you have reasons for thinking, 'I'm not really LGB'?" Twelve of the 20 LGB-identified respondents and 15 of the 34 LGB-dis-identified respondents indicated "yes." Among those *identified* participants who had reasons to deny being LGB, their reasons were as follow: "My family won't approve/love me" (6 of 12 or 50%), "People will hate or reject me" (41.6%), "I am dating someone of the opposite sex" (41.6%), "I am married" (25%), "It doesn't fit my plan for the future" (25%), "I like members of the opposite sex also" (16.6%), "It's just sex, I was experimenting" (16.6%), and "I don't have stereotypical LGB behavior or mannerisms" (16.6%). Five LGB-identified participants offered additional reasons for thinking they might not be LGB; the responses were analyzed and emergent themes included, "Previously married," "Going to hell," and "Haven't met the right person yet" (of opposite sex).

Among the 15 *dis-identified* respondents who indicated reasons to deny being LGB, the most frequently endorsed items were: "I like members of the opposite sex" (9 of 15 or 60%), "My family won't approve/love me" (53.3%), and "People will hate or reject me" (53.3%). Other items included, "It doesn't fit my plan for the future" (33.3%), "I am dating someone of the opposite sex" (26.6%), "I don't have stereotypical LGB behavior or mannerisms" (20%), "It's just sex, I was experimenting" (20%), and "I am married" (6.7%). Nine LGB-dis-identified respondents offered alternative responses to this question; the responses were analyzed and the emergent themes included: "Not admitting it to others, although to self," "Fear of God's rejection," "Denial," "Gender confusion," "Did not want to label self as gay," and "Shame and confusion."

Table 4. *Percentage of Respondents' Answers to the Question, "When You First Began to Think That You Really Were Gay or Lesbian, What Did You Do About It?"*

	Identified	Dis-Identified
"Sought other gay or lesbian individuals."	60.0%	29.4%
"Sought counseling to sort through my confusion."	20.0%	8.0%
"Sought counseling to change my sexual orientation."	5.0%	2.9%
"Sought information in gay or lesbian literature."	45.0%	11.7%
"Sought objective information on homosexuality."	25.0%	11.7%
"Sought same-sex sexual experiences."	60.0%	26.4%
"Sought sexual experiences with members of the opposite sex."	20.0%	0.0%
"Avoided any thoughts or feelings related to feelings of same-sex attraction."	5.0%	14.7%
"Avoided any appearances of homosexuality."	10.0%	23.5%
"Prayed for God to cure me."	30.0%	17.6%
"Talked to my parents."	5.0%	8.8%
"Denied these attractions because of feelings of shame."	20.0%	14.7%
Other	20.0%	11.7%

To continue with the theme of attributions and meaning-making, we also asked, "Before you identified/dis-identified with your feelings of same-sex attraction, did you ever undergo a period when you thought or felt your experiences were due to something other than an LGB identity?" Seven of the 20 LGB-identified respondents and 20 of the 34 dis-identified respondents answered "yes" to this item. Among the 7 LGB-identified respondents, 2 thought that same-sex attraction was related to sexual abuse, and 2 attributed same-sex attraction to personal weakness. One thought same-sex attraction was the result of deficits in parental relationships, and 1 respondent attributed same-sex attraction to emotional dependency. Themes from the additional responses included, "Same-sex attraction unrelated to sexual orientation in childhood," "Sexual play not related to sexual abuse," "Grew up with derogatory terms" (for example, "fag" and "pervert"), and "Not having enough sex."

Among the 20 dis-identified respondents who associated their same-sex attraction to something other than an LGB identity, 11 individuals thought same-sex attraction was the result of deficits in parental relationships, and 10 indicated that their attractions signaled emotional dependency. Nine attributed same-sex attraction to personal weakness and 8 related it to sexual abuse. Six respondents offered an alternative attribution, and of the analyzed responses, emergent themes included, "Did not understand root [cause]," "Emotional problem," "Gender confusion," and "Didn't feel connected to same-sex."

The existence of attributions is indicative of a psychological process, which is a distinguishing feature among both LGB-identified and dis-identified participants. Those who identified as LGB appeared to address their concerns more directly (that is, higher percentages reported this behavior) by seeking out LGB identity-affirming actions (for example, seeking same-sex sexual experiences). We turn now to the potentially natural outgrowth of these attributions. One such consideration is whether a person identified privately (to self only) or publicly identified (to others) as heterosexual. We also asked if, during this time of sexual identity development, participants ever privately or publicly identified as LGB.

Private/Public Identification as Heterosexual and LGB

In our original pilot study 13 of 14 LGB-integrated individuals acknowledged that they had identified themselves as heterosexual at some point in their lives. Four of these 13 were previously married and 1 of these 4 had children—"I was married for 20 years. Until I was 50 years old, I identified as heterosexual, married with kids." Of the dis-identified participants, 12 of 14 had also identified themselves as heterosexual, whereas 3 did not. Two of these 3 participants who did not identify as heterosexual reported being "in process," although they ascribe to a heterosexual role: "I consider myself a heterosexual today, but do not publicly state it. I don't publicly state that I'm gay either. I don't publicly state anything." The other individual provided a description of her current identity:

> I've gone with the ex-gay label because it's the closest thing that is honest. I don't use the term "heterosexual." I am not gay, I don't identify with the political movement. But I am still attracted to people of the same sex. But I don't act out on it because it's not what God wants of me.

Privately identifying as heterosexual was reported by half of the LGB-identified participants in the pilot study. At the time they did not think other options existed. As 1 participant reported, "I never knew that there was anything other than being married and being heterosexual." A number of the participants who did not privately identify as heterosexual stated that they had never consciously wondered about their sexual orientation. "I don't remember saying to myself, 'I am heterosexual'. . . . I went through a heterosexual life, but I don't know that I could say that—I am heterosexual"

Nine dis-identified participants reported that they did identify privately as heterosexual and 3 did not, as they are still in process. One of these participants shared, "No, I never have because the struggle is still so very real to me. It is daily. . . . I choose to not act out . . . and yet still have the images and thoughts in my head."

In the Sexual Identity Project, respondents were asked if, before they achieved their current sexual identity synthesis, there was a time when they identified privately (to self only) as heterosexual. We saw greater between group differences in response to this question, as only 8 of the 20 (40%) LGB-identified participants compared to 25 of the 34 (73.5%) dis-identified participants indicated "yes" to this question (see Table 5).

We also asked about public identification (to others) as heterosexual, and the difference observed in private identification all but disappears with regard to public identification. Sixteen of 20 (80%) of the LGB-identified individuals and 25 of 34 (73.5%) LGB-dis-identified individuals indicated "yes" to this question.

Because we asked about private/public identification as heterosexual, we also asked if, prior to achieving current sexual identity synthesis, there was a time when participants identified privately/publicly as gay or lesbian. Sixteen of 20 (80%) of the LGB-identified respondents compared to only 20 of 34 (58.5%) LGB-dis-identified respondents stated they had identified themselves privately (to self only) as gay or lesbian. When asked about public identification, only 10 of 20 (50%) of the LGB-identified respondents and only 12 of 34 (35.2%) LGB-dis-identified respondents indicated public identification as lesbian or gay during early stages of sexual identity development. Thus, apparently there are various factors that mediate the process of public and private identification as both heterosexual and LGB. The attributions made during the time of sexual identity dilemma may be influential, particularly if initial self-explanations are weighted with religious or parental values that are counter to an LGB identification.

Table 5. *Public/Private Identification as Heterosexual and LGB During Early Stages of Sexual Identity Development*

	Public Identification (to others)		Private Identification (to oneself)	
	LGB-Id	LGB-Dis-Id	LGB-Id	LGB-Dis-Id
as Heterosexual	80%	73.5%	40%	73.5%
as LGB	50%	35.2%	80%	58.5%

Reappraisal of Initial Identification

In our original pilot study in which we interviewed 14 LGB identified individuals, 6 stated they had reconsidered their initial identification as gay or lesbian because of the "cost." For example, 1 interviewee said, "There were still growing pains, growing into a new self" and "I went through a grieving process—turmoil about establishing marriage, families." Six reported never reconsidering their initial decision to identify as

LGB. Three of these individuals indicated that they experienced better relationships with the same-sex than with the opposite sex. For example, 1 interviewee remarked, "Not once. The fit was perfect. Yeah, this is right. Didn't want a relationship at first."

Eleven of the 14 dis-identified interviewees in the pilot study reconsidered their decision to dis-identify; however, some did not engage again in same-sex behavior due to support from their accountability partners (n = 4), and others were prevented by their relationship with God (n = 5). As 1 participant shared, "If I gave up the lifestyle, I gave up everything I knew . . . outside the [gay] community, I felt like a stranger in a strange land." However, it was her spiritual mother's influence that had imparted something to her that prevented her from returning to active same-sex behavior.

In the pilot study we also interviewed the LGB-identified participants about attempts *not* to identify with same-sex attractions; 9 LGB-integrated participants acknowledged that, at one point in their lives, they tried not to identify with same-sex attraction because it "was not easy" (n = 3) or they "did not want it" (n = 2). One of 4 individuals who reported that they did not try to dis-identify with their same-sex attraction averred, "That would be a lie. It would be like trying to live a lie."

Similarly, we asked dis-identified interviewees about attempts to identify with their same-sex attraction, and 8 of the 14 dis-identified participants stated that at one point in their lives, they had tried to identify with their same-sex attraction: "Yeah. I became 'Dykula.' I was the best lesbian there ever was!" For the other 6 dis-identified participants, although they experienced same-sex attraction and even engaged in same-sex relationships, they could not actually identify as homosexual. For example, 1 participant shared, "It's like me 'putting my toe in the water.' Not fully embracing the lifestyle. . . . I couldn't allow myself to do that publicly. Probably a fear of rejection. There was still an identification with the struggle."

In the Sexual Identity Project only 3 of the 20 (15%) LGB-identified participants had reconsidered their LGB identity after their initial decision to identify as LGB. Their reasons for doing so included, "Feelings of guilt and shame" (n = 2), "Lack of support from local church" (n = 2), "Financial cost" (n = 1), and "Lack of support from family" (n = 1).

In contrast, 20 of the 34 (58.8%) dis-identified participants had reconsidered their initial rejection of the "gay" or "lesbian" label. The most frequently cited reason for reconsidering the initial rejection of the

LGB label was "Emotional cost of dis-identifying" (indicated by 12 of 20 respondents, or 60% of those who reconsidered their initial rejection of an LGB label). Other reasons were, "Lack of support from local church" (40%), "Lack of support from friends" (35%), "Lack of support from family" (25%), and "Financial cost" (10%). Several dis-identified individuals offered additional responses, including, "Counsel to just say 'no' to homosexuality," "Feelings of same-sex attraction remained," "Desire for emotional closeness," "Not having community," "Inability to stop sexual encounters," and "Sexual frustration."

To pinpoint the issue of reconsidering one's identity from another angle, we asked LGB-identified participants if they had ever tried to *not* identify with their same-sex attraction. Eight of 20 (40%) indicated "yes" to this question, and the most frequently cited reasons for not identifying were, "Because I didn't want to live as an outcast" (100%), "It was not easy" (37.5%), and "Because I didn't want to be in the lifestyle" (37.5%). Additional themes included fear of hell, one's family, and thinking there were no other individuals with similar experiences.

We asked the parallel, yet converse, question to those who dis-identified: Did you ever actively try to identify with your experiences of same-sex attraction? Twenty-five of 34 (73.5%) indicated "yes" to this question. The most common reasons given for trying to identify with experiences of same-sex attraction included, "It was easier to (emotionally, relationally)" (60%) and "Didn't think I had a choice" (52%). Additional themes included satisfaction of emotional needs and sexual desire.

To follow-up these questions, we asked those who had reconsidered their sexual identity to indicate what helped them adopt their current sexual identity. Among those who reported re-thinking their decision to identify as LGB, they unanimously indicated, "More fulfilling intimate relationships with members of the same sex" and "My relationship with God." One other participant noted the "Emotional cost of not being in the lifestyle."

Among the dis-identified participants, those who reconsidered their decision to dis-identify, but ultimately chose to dis-identify, indicated that their "relationship with God" was the most frequently cited reason to adopt their current identity (95%). This factor was followed by "Accountability" (65%), "Emotional cost of participating in the lifestyle" (45%), "Lack of support from local church" (20%), "Lack of support from family" (15%), "Lack of support from friends" (15%), and "Financial cost" (10%). Additional reasons given included, "Help from Christian counselor," "Encouragement from ex-gay believer," "Understood roots of homosexuality," "Marital covenant," "Knowing who I am," and "Knew it was wrong, couldn't continue living like that."

There appear to be a number of factors that influence this sample's experience of sexual identity development, made manifest in shared experience between groups, as well as noted differences. We will next discuss the themes and psychological processes reported during sexual identity development.

Discussion of Themes and Psychological Processes

We turn our attention now to the salient themes and psychological processes evident from the study. Figure 1 illustrates these themes and processes and is our reference point for discussion of the following: lack of LGB-affirming responses, the important of like-minded others, attributions about what same-sex attractions signal, and reappraisal of efforts to make sense of experiences of same-sex attraction.

Lack of LGB-Affirming Responses

A first observation is the rarity for either LGB-identified or LGB-disidentified individuals to recall an LGB-affirmative response to their own experience of tension or confusion about same-sex attraction. Only 2 of the 20 LGB-identified and only 3 of the 34 LGB dis-identified individuals attributed their same-sex attraction to who they "really are" as a person. Although it was more common for LGB-dis-identified individuals to attribute same-sex attraction to a "passing phase," both groups initially tended to think something was "wrong" with them.

A much higher percentage (65%) of LGB-identified participants (compared to 38% of dis-identified participants) initially thought their same-sex attraction meant they were gay or lesbian. By self-report they were more likely to make the self-defining attribution, "I am gay/lesbian." The majority of dis-identified individuals did not report making this self-defining attribution. Those who dis-identified were more likely to attribute experiences of same-sex attraction to the desire to be close to the same sex or the desire to be loved.

The difficulty with this interpretation is the retrospective nature of this research. Perhaps the dis-identified respondents may, at one point

Figure 1. Themes Characteristic of Sexual Identity Development

Initial attempts to make meaning	Initial response	Identification	Reappraisal
LGB-Identified			
Something is wrong with me (40%)	Sought other LGB persons (60%)	Private-as heterosexual (40%)	Yes (15%)
Different sex (30%)	Sought same-sex experiences (60%)	as LGB (80%)	-guilt/shame
I am damaged (20%)	Information in LGB literature (45%)	Public -as heterosexual (80%)	-lack of support
		-as LGB (50%)	
LGB-Dis-Identified			
Something is wrong with me (59%)	Sought other LGB persons (29%)	Private-as heterosexual (74%)	Yes (59%)
A passing phase (35%)	Sought same-sex experiences (26%)	-as LGB (59%)	-emotional cost
Different sex (24%)		Public -as heterosexual (74%)	-lack of support
I am damaged (21%)		-as LGB (35%)	

have told themselves, "I am gay/lesbian;" however, in light of their current sexual identification, attributions of a less declarative nature may be recalled with greater clarity. Likewise, gay-affirmative attributions may have been reported with higher frequency by LGB-identified individuals because those thoughts, feelings and experiences are more congruent with their current identity.

Like-Minded Others

Upon first making the connection between themselves and an LGB identity, the identified individuals tended to seek others who shared their LGB identity and engage in same-sex behavior. Only one-fourth of the dis-identified individuals reported "seeking those who identified as LGB" or "seeking same-sex behavior." Dis-identified individuals appeared to avoid the issue of same-sex attraction in greater proportion than the LGB-identified participants. For example, 14.7% of dis-identified individuals (compared with 5% of LGB-identified) stated that they "avoided any thoughts or feelings related to feelings of same-sex attraction." Likewise, 23.5% (compared with 10% of LGB-identified individuals) "avoided any appearances of homosexuality." This suggests that behavior constraints, such as religious or parental values, may have been more influential at the outset of the sexual identity dilemma for dis-identified participants.

Identity Attributions

Both groups reported struggling with thinking they were not really LGB. Desire for the opposite sex and fear of rejection were both noted, as well as concerns about family members' reactions. This fear is often reported in sexual identity development literature.[11]

Some early attributions about same-sex attraction are also noteworthy.[12] Among LGB-identified participants, although 2 mentioned past sexual abuse and 2 mentioned personal weakness, no theme stands apart with respect to attributions about same-sex attraction. In contrast, dis-identified participants tended to attribute same-sex attraction to deficits in parent-child relationships and emotional dependency. Put differently, those who dis-identified with an LGB-ideology attributed more negative causes or stigmatizing experiences to origins of same-sex attraction than those who integrated their experiences of same-sex attraction into an LGB identity. One possible explanation is that these attributions were articulated from a specific valuative framework, but there may be other interpretations, perhaps including the view that "sinful" behaviors have "sinful" origins, although this would require further study.

We noted, too, that the two groups had markedly different responses with respect to private identification (to self only) as heterosexual. Only 40% of the LGBs compared to 74% of the dis-identified indicated private self-identification as heterosexual. But public identification was a different matter: both groups admitted to a public identification as heterosexual (80% of LGB and 74% of those who dis-identified). This greater proportion of public identification as heterosexual speaks to the power of societal norms on individual sexuality.

Perhaps the private/public identification is most significant when identifying oneself (to self only) early on as gay or lesbian. Eighty percent of the LGB-identified respondents compared to only 59% of those who later dis-identified identified privately (to self only) as gay or lesbian. When asked about public identification, half of the LGB-identified respondents reported public identification, compared to only 35% of LGB-dis-identified respondents. When we consider these early stages of sexual identity development, we may discover that the "tapes" running in a person's mind influence how they regard themselves (privately) and how they express themselves (publicly) to others. This speaks to attributions and meaning-making. For reasons not entirely clear, LGB-identified participants were more likely to recall identifying privately as LGB. A smaller (though significant) percentage of dis-identified participants did not make this attribution.

Research suggests that disclosure of an LGB identity occurs on average about 2 years after self-labeling, and, as Dube and Savin-Williams suggest,[13] many believe that "public avowal fortifies sexual identity." Disclosure can certainly also place a person at risk of being rejected by others.

Identity Reappraisal

It is interesting to contrast the reports of reconsidering one's initial decision to identify or dis-identify with an LGB identity. Only 15% of LGB respondents reported reconsidering their initial decision—compared to almost 59% of the dis-identified respondents. "Lack of support from local church" was a common reason cited by dis-identified respondents (and also by 1 of the 3 identified participants). Other groups failing to offer adequate support included family members and friends. Interestingly, financial cost was not as great a concern for many people, despite the high cost of therapy and long-term commitment to a course of treatment.[14]

Relatively few LGB participants reported reconsidering their initial decision to identify as LGB, as compared to the dis-identified participants, who reported reconsidering their initial decision to dis-identify. Whether this suggests that the pathway to dis-identification is more difficult, or if there is less support for dis-identification is unclear. Although society is growing increasingly tolerant of those who identify as LGB, many in the LGB community might disagree that there is nearly the support for an LGB identity synthesis as for dis-identification. However, those in the dis-identified community would declare that, although there is the expectation that dis-identification is possible, few resources are available to assist in this transition. "Support" thus tends to be a nominal exercise instead of a practical one.

There is not much extant research on the decision to pursue one identity synthesis over another. In Schaeffer et al.'s[15] one-year follow-up of individuals pursuing change of behavior or orientation (seen in the context of the broader construct of sexual identity), 4.3% of those surveyed were unsure whether to continue their efforts to change (whereas 132 of 140 [94.3%] of participants reported they were still attempting to change [n = 91] or had changed [n = 41] their orientation).

Perhaps in the future researchers will find that behavioral success predicts an individual's decision about a specific course of sexual identity development. In the Schaeffer et al. study, 89 of 140 (63.6%) participants in a follow-up study reported behavioral success, that is, they were able to avoid engaging in same-sex behavior (60.8% of males; n = 62 and 71.1% of females; n = 27), yet the vast majority (88.2%) were still attempting change. To follow these participants over the course of the next several years and note the relationship between behavioral success and identity reappraisal would be an important endeavor. A much smaller percentage (1.4%; n = 2) were no longer attempting to change their orientation.[16]

Chapter 6

Sexual Identity Synthesis

Introduction

"Ben," age 21, came to counseling at the request of his mother. She stated that she "never would have in a million years" thought that he was gay, yet he came home from college for the summer and "came out" to his family. She wanted to help him, but more than anything she wanted him to understand why she could not accept his identity. Ben reported feeling "different" from others since childhood. He stated that he dated the opposite sex because it was expected, but that he never really felt emotionally connected to the young women he dated. He said that for the first time he was comfortable with his identity, and that his coming out was really an expression of his "true self."

—authors' files

"Sarah," age 35, agreed to meet for a consultation regarding her sexual identity. She reported that at a young age she really did not feel "different" the way many in the gay community suggest, but by puberty did not find herself sharing an interest in boys. She reported a stronger emotional connection to girls that developed over the years and might be referred to as "sexual," though she describes it more as emotional longing and preoccupation with others. Sarah does not talk as much about whether orientation can be changed. She has not had success in getting rid of all of her same-sex attractions, but she is satisfied with her quality of life and she reports not being bothered by them anymore. Some days they occupy her mind more, but most days they seem more manageable and she is comfortable with both a private and public identity as heterosexual.

—authors' files

As Ben and Sarah's stories suggest, those who are satisfied with their sexual identity proceed with either of two broad directions. The first direction is highlighted by other broader models of lesbian, gay or bisexual (LGB) identity development, and is often demonstrated by sexual exploration, disclosure, or expansion of cultural contacts.[1] Indeed, there are numerous studies depicting the experiences of LGB persons who have achieved identity synthesis. For example, Troiden[2] reports that the final stage of sexual identity synthesis, which he refers to as *Commitment*, is characterized by a sense of pride in one's homosexuality, and viewed as normal and natural. Coleman[3] refers to this as *Integration*, and Grace[4] refers to this as *Self-Definition and Reintegration*. In McDonald's model,[5] sexual identity synthesis is the culmination of seven stages, the last of which is referred to as a *Positive Gay Identity*. Among models of lesbian identity development and synthesis, Chapman and Brannock[6] designated these experiences as *Self-Identification*, and Sophie[7] labeled it a time of *Identity Integration*, which is attained as a woman integrates her same-sex attraction into other aspects of her identity to create a more stable self.

Although not an examination of sexual identity synthesis *per se*, Shidlo and Schroeder[8] recently published a study documenting self-perceived gay identity synthesis following failed attempts to change sexual orientation.[9] Among those who integrated their experiences of same-sex attraction into an LGB identity synthesis following therapy, two groups emerged: (1) those who reported long-term negative consequences (including self-blame and confusion) from involvement in therapy and (2) those who reported resilience or "psychological hardiness" following therapy. The latter group reported feeling "strengthened by their experience of having tried to change."[10]

The second or alternative broad trajectory is away from an LGB identity synthesis, also referred to by some as a "heterosexual shift"; whereas others describe it as simply a resumption of personal development articulated within a valuative frame of reference about sexual behavior. In the Schaeffer et al.[11] one-year follow-up of individuals pursuing change of behavior or orientation,[12] all participants reported some degree of religious motivatation; however, high religious motivation predicted behavioral success (defined as abstaining from engaging in same-sex sexual behaviors, despite same-sex attraction). Among those who had behavioral success, higher self-reported levels of happiness and self-acceptance were noted, along with lower levels of loneliness, depression, guilt, and paranoia. Similarly, Spitzer[13] reported on 200 homosexuals who claimed to have made a significant shift toward heterosexuality (or what we might refer to in some cases as an alternative identity synthesis) and found that his sample was more likely to be "markedly" or "extremely" depressed *before* their change attempt (43% of males; 47% of females) rather than *after* (1% of males; 4% of females).

These findings regarding measures of mental health are probably true whether a person pursues an LGB identity synthesis or if they disidentify with an LGB identity.[14] In an unpublished study comparing gay and lesbians and "ex-gays," Nottebaum, Schaeffer, Rood, and Leffler[15] report positive mental health in their identity synthesis, with gay and lesbian participants reporting greater happiness, self-acceptance, and less loneliness and paranoia. Perhaps on measures of happiness or self-acceptance, it matters most not whether a person pursues a particular path of identity synthesis but whether their identity synthesis is *congruent* with their broader valuative framework. The pathway to congruence is worthy of further exploration. One's coping skills, experience of social support, and other resources probably helps to move toward congruence, as self-attitude comes to reflect how one lives. Thus, it appears that congruence between an individual's worldview and his or her perception of how sexual identity fits within that framework resolves the cognitive dissonance.

What is particularly interesting in the Sexual Identity Project is that both groups identify as Christian. Christianity, like all other major religions,[16] has historically rejected same-sex behavior as indisputably immoral. In other words, no distinction is made between same-sex behavior occurring in a loving, monogamous relationship—or in a series of quick encounters with anonymous sex partners. Not surprisingly then, bringing together Christianity and experiences of same-sex attraction is particularly challenging for those who are inexplicably attracted to the same sex. In an interesting ethnographic study of 16 members of the United Fellowship of Metropolitan Community Churches and 14 members of Exodus ministries, Wolkomir[17] found an "ideological conflict" with traditional Christianity. We will see in this chapter how our participants report on their encounter with this conflict as they share their memories of attaining a sexual identity synthesis.

We begin by asking about constraints to sexual identity synthesis. We wanted to know which obstacles, if any, people recalled as they traveled toward congruence. Conversely, we also wanted to learn more about specific experiences that facilitated sexual identity synthesis. What motivated them along the path toward synthesis of their sexual identity? Because we had specifically looked for a religious sample, we also asked several questions about the relationship between religion and sexual identity synthesis.

The Sexual Identity Project

Age at Identity Synthesis

These reports are comparable to our pilot study findings, in which the mean age for LGB integrated participants when they synthesized their same-sex attractions into an LGB identity was 24.5 years (range = 16-50 years; SD = 9.0). Dis-identified interviewees from our original pilot study reported achieving an alternative sexual identity (i.e., dis-identified from their experiences of same-sex attraction and achieved an alternative sexual identity synthesis) at a mean age of 28 years (range = 16-43 years; SD = 7.8).

In the larger study, the average age at which time those who integrated their experiences into an LGB identity synthesis recalled doing so was 24.8 years (SD = 7.2) for males and 27.9 years (SD = 13.1) for females. Among those who dis-identified with an LGB identity synthesis, the average age of achieving an alternative identity synthesis was 33.3 years (SD = 5.7 for males and 34.3 years (SD = 12.5) for females.

Initial examination of the data for the sexual identity project raised the question of whether there are differences between members of the LGB-identified and LGB-dis-identified populations regarding age at identity synthesis. Statistical analysis does reveal a significant difference, with the LGB-identified individuals averaging identity synthesis at 25.9 years (range = 9-55 years; SD = 9.54) and dis-identified participants doing so at 33.7 years (range = 17 to 60, SD = 9.16) ($F(1, 51) = 8.56$, $p = .005$). Thus, dis-identified participants tended to be older than LGB identified participants when they synthesized their current sexual identities.

Constraints to Synthesis

We wanted to gather information on constraints that once prevented individuals from achieving their current sexual identity synthesis. In other words, whether one identified currently as LGB, or dis-identified privately and publicly with an LGB identity, we wanted to increase our understanding of which obstacles they encountered enroute to a fuller sexual identity synthesis.

In our original pilot study we interviewed both LGB-identified and LGB dis-identified individuals about hindrances or constraints. Several reasons were cited by LGB-identified participants as stumbling blocks to their identification: 4 individuals noted the stigma/shame of homosexuality; 7 mentioned family relationships (e.g., "Letting my father down—because my father believes in Catholicism strongly. It was against his beliefs."); 2 reported peer influence; 3 were influenced by denial/hiding; 5 were afraid that the church or God would reject them (e.g., "Religiously, I wondered if God would send me to Hell. It made me hate my own insides."); and 1 LGB integrated person mentioned sexual abuse (e.g., "My uncle's molestation. . . . I had to put love and sex together because of that. I had to accept that someone would love me and want to have sex with me.").

We had asked similar questions of the dis-identified interviewees. Ten of the 14 dis-identified participants had difficulty dis-identifying with their same-sex attraction because their emotional needs were being met in current same-sex relationships. For example, one female participant shared: "People I was attracted to were my best friends. Whoever I was close to, they became my object of attraction. . . . The hardest thing was my realization that I was leaving a person behind. It wasn't just sexual." Four dis-identified participants acknowledged that being in the "lifestyle"[18] met their physical and sexual needs. Another 4 stated that being in the lifestyle suited their selfhood perfectly; for example, one participant shared, "The gay lifestyle was a perfect fit. It agreed with all my personal theology. I was a 'human doing' and my partner was a 'human being.'" Three dis-identified individuals reported being hindered in their pursuit of dis-identification because they had not known others who had undergone the process.

In the larger study we specifically asked, "Before fully identifying/dis-identifying with same-sex attractions, what hindered this process?" When asked about various potential constraints, respondents could choose from options derived from the content analysis of the original pilot study. Themes drawn from that analysis for the LGB-identified respondents were, "The effects of sexual abuse," "The stigma of homosexuality in society," "Negative family relationships," "Negative peer relationships," "Fear of hurting my family," "Denial of my feelings of same-sex attraction," "Emotional cost (loss of support)," "and Spiritual cost (fear that church/God would reject me)."

Table 1. *Percentage of LGB-Identified Respondents' Answers to the Question, "Before You Fully Identified and Achieved Your Current Sexual Identity Synthesis with Your Experiences of Same-Sex Attractions . . . , What Hindered This Process?"*

	Percentage
"The effects of sexual abuse."	0
"The stigma of homosexuality in society."	80
"Negative family relationships."	50
"Negative peer relationships."	40
"Fear of hurting my family."	60
"Denial of my feelings of same-sex attraction."	30
"Emotional cost (loss of support)."	30
"Spiritual cost (for example, fear that the church/religion, God would reject me)"	50
Other	20

Those who integrated their experiences of same-sex attraction into an LGB identity synthesis indicated a range of responses, although clearly the most often indicated constraint was the stigma associated with an LGB identity, as 16 of 20 (80%) identified "The stigma of homosexuality in society" as a constraint. Other more frequently endorsed items included, "Fear of hurting my family" (60%), "Negative family relationships" (50%), and "Spiritual cost (fear that church/God would reject me)" (50%). Additional obstructions included, "Negative peer relationships" (40%), "Denial of my feelings of same-sex attraction" (30%), and "Emotional cost (loss of support)" (30%). None of the LGB-identified respondents indicated that effects of sexual abuse had hindered the process of fully identifying as LGB. This response is inconsistent with a common assumption that early experiences of sexual abuse "cause" a person to feel same-sex attraction. Although this study does not address that question directly, sexual abuse was not identified by this sample of LGB individuals as a stumbling block to current sexual identity. Four LGB-identified respondents offered additional hindrances. The themes arising from their responses were, "Loss of money or income," "Persecution" (e.g., "witch hunts" in the military), and "Didn't meet another LGB person until later."

Table 2. *Percentage of LGB-Dis-Identified Respondents' Answers to the Question, "Before You Fully Identified and Achieved Your Current Sexual Identity Synthesis with Your Experiences of Same-Sex Attractions . . . , What Hindered This Process?"*

	Percentage
"My emotional needs were met in a homosexual relationship."	47.1
"Being in the lifestyle met my desire/lust."	47.1
"I felt the lifestyle fit my sense of being/selfhood perfectly."	20.6
"Emotional cost (loss of support)."	20.6
"I didn't know anyone who 'dis-identified.'"	29.4
"Feelings of ambivalence."	32.4
Other	44.1

We contrasted LGB-identified responses with those of LGB-dis-identified respondents, who also chose from options derived from the content analysis of the original pilot study. These options included, "Emotional needs met in homosexual relationships," "Being in the lifestyle met my desire/lust," "Felt the lifestyle fit my sense of being/selfhood perfectly," "Emotional cost (loss of support)," "I didn't know anyone who 'dis-identified,'" and "Feelings of ambivalence."

When asked about specific constraints to their LGB-dis-identified sexual identity synthesis, the highest percentages of respondents indicated that emotional needs were being met in a homosexual relationship (47.1%) or that being in the lifestyle met their desire/lust (47.1%). Other endorsed items included, "Feelings of ambivalence" (32.4%), "I didn't know anyone who 'dis-identified'" (29.4%), "Felt the lifestyle fit my sense of being/personhood perfectly" (20.6%), and "Emotional cost (loss of support)" (20.6%). Fifteen LGB-dis-identified respondents offered additional constraints; these responses were analyzed for themes, which included, "Did not have the skills/did not know how to dis-identify," "Fear" (of unknown and of failure), "No one would understand," "Doubt about physical intimacy with opposite sex," "Laziness," and "Thought I was 'born that way.'"

So there are indeed various constraints identified by both LGB-identified and dis-identified individuals from the study that had impeded their current sexual identification. These constraints differ for each group as each works toward a different end state. As we consider the outcome, that is, the process of sexual identity synthesis, we next discuss experiences recalled by participants that facilitated identity integration.

Experiences that Facilitated Synthesis

In addition to constraints, we also wanted to better understand experiences that facilitated participants' current sexual identity synthesis. We wanted to know if specific experiences or relationships seemed to assist them in the attainment of their current sexual identity. Again, it may be helpful to understand how the pilot data informed our questions in this portion of the questionnaire. Four LGB integrated interviewees from the pilot study were encouraged to identify with their experiences of same-sex attraction because they had met others actively involved in a gay community. As one participant reported, "When I finally found a gay community, that helped a lot. I stopped wanting to die. Maybe someone will accept me." Being in a personal relationship with someone of the same-sex also encouraged 4 individuals to identify.

For 4 others, it was the *experience* of same-sex behavior or same-sex attraction that facilitated this identification. Three LGB participants stated that being on the verge of a psychological crisis perpetuated the need to act, which for them, meant identifying—"Feeling of absolutely losing my mind . . . it had to be reconciled. . . . I needed to reconcile this for my psychological well-being."

In contrast to those who identified with their experiences of same-sex attraction, 5 dis-identified interviewees from the initial pilot study found encouragement to dis-identify from their mentors or accountability partners. Programs such as Living Waters enabled 3 individuals to sever connections to the gay community. Eight dis-identified participants reported belief in God, or what they perceived to be God's presence or intervention, as a factor in their dis-identification. As 1 dis-identified participant put it: "My faith. That was the first thing that encouraged me to change. God was powerful enough to pull me out of it." Finding the same-sex relationships unfulfilling or painful motivated 5 individuals to dis-identify. One member shared, "How dissatisfied I was with it when I really embraced it. My lover didn't fulfill what I needed . . . it was just sexual desire for me, not a connection that I was seeking."

From our interviews with LGB-identified and dis-identified individuals in the pilot study, we asked the following question: "Before fully identifying/dis-identifying with same-sex attraction, what encouraged this process?" Sixteen of 20 (80%) indicated that current feelings of same-sex attraction facilitated sexual identity synthesis as LGB. Other more common experiences that encouraged an LGB identity synthesis included, "Having contacts with the gay or lesbian community" (65%), "An intimate and personal relationship with someone of the same sex" (60%), Experiences or sexual behavior with someone of the same sex" (55%). Less frequently noted experiences which helped ease the transition toward an LGB identity synthesis included, "Psychological crisis" (20%) and "Having a family member who is gay or lesbian" (5%). Three LGB-identified respondents offered additional experiences that facilitated an LGB identity synthesis such as, "Dated same sex secretly," "Considered suicide," and "Wanted to live life honestly" (see Table 3).

Table 3. *Percentage of LGB-Identified Respondents' Answers to the Question, "Before You Fully Identified and Achieved Your Current Sexual Identity Synthesis with Your Experiences of Same-Sex Attractions . . . , What* **Encouraged** *This Process?"*

	Percentage
"Having contacts in the gay or lesbian community."	65
"An intimate and personal relationship with someone of the same sex."	60
"Having a family member who is gay or lesbian."	5
"Feelings of same-sex attraction."	80
"Experience or sexual behavior with someone of the same sex."	55
"Psychological crisis (that is, "If I don't, I'm going to die")."	20
Other	15

Among the LGB-dis-identified respondents, "God's intervention" was the most frequently endorsed item (88.2%), followed by "Conviction of the Holy Spirit" (76.5%), Programs such as Living Waters or other curriculum . . . that supported me in leaving the lifestyle" (64.7%), "Being in the lifestyle was unfulfilling or painful" (58.8%), and "People in my life encouraged me to leave the lifestyle" (44.1%). A number of LGB-dis-identified individuals offered additional reasons, which helped to facilitate their sexual identity synthesis. The responses were analyzed and the following themes emerged as particularly salient: "Turned to God/Obedience to God," "Realized change was possible/wanted change," "Condemnation from friends/Bible," "Exodus support group," "Testimonies from ex-gays," and "Social support" (see Table 4).

Because we deliberately searched for religiously-affiliated groups, we asked how a religious/spiritual worldview helped to facilitate their

Table 4. *Percentage of LGB-Dis-Identified Respondents' Answers to the Question, "Before You Fully Identified and Achieved Your Current Sexual Identity Synthesis with Your Experiences of Same-Sex Attractions . . . , What* **Encouraged** *This Process?"*

	Percentage
"God's intervention (for example, conviction)."	88.2
"Being in the lifestyle was unfulfilling or painful."	58.8
"Programs such as Living Waters or other curriculum from an Exodus group supported me in leaving the lifestyle."	64.7
"People in my life encouraged me to leave the lifestyle (for example, mentors, accountability partner)."	44.1
"Conviction of the Holy Spirit."	76.5
Other	58.8

sexual identity, particularly if they had ever been re-thinking their sexual identity. Among the LGB-identified respondents, 35% reported that "it didn't help or enter the picture" and 20% indicated that they were not "accepted in church." The same percentage (20%) of respondents remarked that their spiritual worldview helped them "cope by seeking out a supportive spiritual community," and 20% also reported seeking the Lord in prayer and worship." Eight respondents offered additional responses to this question, and emergent themes included, "Avoided or left church" (because it was damaging), "Realized God created me as I am," "Never discussed sexual orientation," "Never thought God did not love me because of sexual orientation," and "Went to church at other's insistence."

Among LGB-dis-identified respondents, a religious/spiritual worldview was highlighted as helpful when re-thinking the decision to identify by seeking the Lord in prayer and worship (88.2%), helping the person cope by seeking a supportive spiritual community (76.4%), and realizing that their religion and a gay or lesbian identity were in contradiction (73.5%). All LGB-dis-identified respondents indicated that their religious/spiritual worldview did assist in their process toward meaning-making and sexual identity synthesis. Six of the respondents, however, offered additional responses, and emergent themes included, "God's love/ plan," "Began getting rid of 'lesbian' label," and "Quit homosexual relationship 10 years prior to spiritual community."

In our original pilot study we posed a more general question about the transition from possibly being LGB, to feeling certain that one was LGB. For LGB-identified interviewees, several significant means arose by which they proceeded from regarding themselves as "possibly" LGB, to identifying as LGB with certainty. Six interviewees claimed that their first relationship facilitated this process. One revealed, "The deciding factor was when I made love to a woman for the first time. You kiss them . . . you cross a boundary you can't get back from." For 7 others, acceptance of their same-sex attraction was indicative of an authenticity of self: "Coming to terms with it, I finally got tired of being dishonest when I was 21 and tired of God not changing me." Three LGB interviewees from the pilot study understood that affirmation of community was instrumental to their identification. Realizing that same-sex attraction felt natural was an approach that 2 LGB participants found helpful in their identity synthesis—"Confirmation came for me when . . . I found happiness or contentment . . . being with a woman . . . it was just the knowledge of knowing. . . . Every time I chose to do what was natural, it felt like confirmation."

When asked during the pilot interviews about the process of regarding self as possibly not LGB to certainly "not LGB," 4 interviewees mentioned that having their gender identity affirmed helped them to pursue an alternative sexual identity not dependent on same-sex attraction. As 1 participant revealed, "I made lots of choices . . . choices for my femininity and for what God had intended me to be. I wanted to know what God had made women for and how He created them. . . ." Six dis-identified interviewees shared that despite feelings of same-sex attraction, they realized that they could not accept those feelings. For example, 1 interviewee stated, "I still struggle with same-sex attraction, but I don't want to be labelled a lesbian. . . . I've been trying to make a different identity for myself . . . it's a process . . . heterosexuality is a by-product of pursuing God." Nine dis-identified individuals cited that

God's ability to meet their needs facilitated the process for them: "The process started with being secure in who I was in God's love. . . . Once secure, I started becoming rooted in who I am as a man of God among other men . . . then there was an attraction to femininity. . . ." However, for 4 of the dis-identified participants, the process of dis-identification is still underway. As 1 participant shared, "I don't believe I am gay. . . . I believe I'm not fully in touch with my masculinity."

We asked participants in the present study about this process. Among the LGB-identified, the most frequently endorsed items from this question were, "It felt natural to me" (70%), "I always knew" (60%), "My first sexual relationship with a member of the same sex" (55%), and "My first emotional relationship with a member of the same sex" (50%). Less frequently confirmed items included, "I accepted my experience of same-sex attraction as who I really am" (40%), and "The gay, lesbian, and bisexual community supported me" (30%).

Likewise, dis-identified participants were asked what moved them from thinking they were possibly not LGB to identifying certainly as "not LGB." The most frequently endorsed items were, "I was obedient to God's calling on my life" (67.6%), "God met my emotional needs" (61.7%), "Gender identity affirmation" (58.8%), and "I am still in process—I am still being transformed" (58.8%). Less frequently confirmed items included, "I learned not to trust my feelings" (44.1%) and "I was dissatisfied with the relationship" (14.7%). Additional themes emergent from the qualitative data included, "Truth of Bible/God," "Not sexualizing friendships/not becoming emotionally dependent," "Awareness of struggle," "My will to not go back," and "God changing my emotional needs."

Emotional Reactions to Sexual Identity

Although we did not include measures of emotional well-being or psychological distress, we did want to gain understanding of participants' emotional reactions to their sexual identity. We asked about feelings that came up when the LGB-identified respondents accepted an LGB identity. Among those identifying as LGB, what might be called positive feelings included "Self-acceptance" (75%), "Relief" (65%), "Peace" (65%), and "Joy" (55%), while negative emotions included "Fear" (50%), "Sadness" (20%), and "Anger" (15%).

Similar emotions were reported by those who initially dis-identified with an LGB identity synthesis. Upon dis-identification, positive emotions included, "Relief" (44.1%), "Peace" (35.2%), "Joy" (29.4%), "Self-acceptance" (23.5%), and "Encouragement" (17.6%). Negative emotions included "Fear" (32.3%), "Sadness" (32.3%), and "Anger" (17.6%). We asked those who dis-identified about their current feelings; fewer respondents experienced negative emotions (e.g., no respondent indicated feeling sad or angry, although 5.9% still felt fear). Higher percentages of current positive emotions were given, e.g., "Peace" (55.8%) and "Joy" (50%).

Along these lines we also asked participants about their happiness at the time of the study (see Table 5). As a rough gauge of one's sense of happiness, we asked participants, "Taken altogether, how would you say things are these days—would you say you are *very happy*, *pretty happy*, or *not too happy*? Seventy-five percent (n = 15 of 20) of the LGB-identified participants indicated they were *very happy*, compared to 52.9% (n = 18 of 34) of the dis-identified sample. Twenty-five percent (n = 5) of the LGB-identified individuals indicated feeling *pretty happy*, compared to 35.2% (18 of 34) of the dis-identified participants. None of the LGB participants and only 2 (5.8%) of the dis-identified participants reported feeling *not too happy*.

Table 5. *Percentage of LGB-Identified and Dis-Identified Respondents' Answers to the Question, "Taken Altogether, How Would You Say Things Are These Days—Would You Say You Are* **Very Happy, Pretty Happy,** *or* **Not Too Happy?***"*

	Identified	Dis-Identified
"Very Happy."	75.0%	52.9%
"Pretty Happy."	25.0%	35.2%
"Not Too Happy."	0.0%	5.8%

Participants were also asked which factors contributed to their rating of happiness, and the emergent themes for LGB individuals included self-acceptance (n = 8), LGB faith community (n = 6), having a committed relationship (n = 4), family (n = 3), and having a community (n = 3). In contrast, dis-identified participants tended to discuss their relationship with God (n = 16), while a smaller number mentioned other factors, such as having dealt with the root causes of same-sex attraction, telling others about their struggle, and having good/healthy friendships.

Religion and Sexual Identity

In part because we have two samples drawn from religious populations, we asked additional questions about participants' religious and spiritual worldview and how it helped them identify (or dis-identify), as well as how it is viewed as a potential coping resource. When asked, "How did your religious or spiritual worldview help you to accept and synthesize your current sexual identity," the most frequently-cited response among those who reported an LGB identity was honesty: "My faith is based on truth, and denying my gay or lesbian identity would be contrary to that truth" (65%). Others reported that their faith gave them "strength to persevere" (20%), while 15% indicated that their faith was no help at all. Another important support that their faith provided was community; for example, one LGB-identified respondent stated,

> MCC has been a wonderful, positive and supportive place to help me in continuing my journey on to becoming comfortable with my faith and sexuality. It has been the first place that I can say has been a consistent place available for support. It has been my family that isn't afraid to share, open up and trust and love each other for who we are as a man or woman who has a lifestyle in common.

When we asked this question of those who dis-identified with an LGB identity, the most prominent theme again was truth: "My faith is based on truth and accepting an LGB identity would be contrary to that truth" (91.1%). Other responses included, "My faith gave me strength to persevere" (67.6%) and "I prayed for a new sexual identity" (44.1%). Additional themes included "Prayer," "Fellowship with other strugglers," and "Freedom from guilt and shame." As one dis-identified participant stated,

> My faith in Jesus has allowed Him into my life to heal wounded areas. With healing comes strength and maturity—which enabled me to grow up and out of the SSA. And if I do have fleeting moments of SSA—I

remember why it happened, and I think of God and who I am in Him.
I can let go of the attraction and move on and be at peace. Amen!

Religion and spirituality were also highlighted as resources for dealing
with the stress and tension associated with identification. When asked
about this, LGB-identified participants tended to emphasize faith (30%)
and the words of Scripture (25%) as a reason to persevere, the allevia-
tion of stress through corporate worship (25%), and the use of prayer in
helping strengthen and comfort (25%).

Dis-identified participants reported similar themes. For example, the
most frequently confirmed item dealt with prayer for strength and comfort (76.4%), followed by having faith (61.7%) and Scripture (73.5%)
provide a reason to persevere. Corporate worship was also indicated as a
resource for alleviating stress, anxiety, or tension by 55.8% of the sample.

Subsequent to the question about how faith and religion helped them
to accept and synthesize their current sexual identities, we asked how
faith and religion hindered or hurt them. Responses to this question were
similar among LGB-identified and dis-identified participants. Twenty
percent of participants who identified as LGB remarked that they had not
been accepted by their church. Likewise, 26.5% of dis-identified group
members had been taught " in church that "God hates homosexuals," or
that they had been shamed and condemned. Secrecy in dealing with same-
sex attraction was noted by a couple dis-identified participants,

> When I was a child, my church was very legalistic and I didn't see
> room for the grace of God to work. I was afraid to confess SSA to
> anyone. I kept it hidden for 40 years from all but one person. I could
> have found help at a younger age if it had been openly offered.

Because this sample is on the "front lines" of the controversial issue of
LGB concerns and the church, we asked how the local church or religious community provided support to individuals who experience same-
sex attraction. Once again the answers can be contrasted, as the themes
arising from the LGB individuals' responses included, "Accurate interpretation of Scripture" (n = 5), "Encourage unconditional love and acceptance" (n = 4), "Realize that God created and loves all of us" (n = 3),
"Sex-positive attitudes preached from the pulpit" (n = 2), "reach out to
homosexuals" (n = 2), and "Increase awareness of homosexuality"
(n = 2). One LGB-identified participant responded with, "Make a conscious effort to reach out to homosexuals, not just tolerate them. In-

crease awareness of hetero-Christians as to who and what we are," and another stated, "Stop the condemnation. If my Southern Baptist church had been more accepting, then my family and non-gay friends would also have been accepting."

When asked about local church or religious community support, participants who dis-identified focused on other concerns. The themes included, "Mentoring, support groups, accountability in the church" (n = 12), "Help church to love, not condemn" (n = 9), "Educate church members about roots, incidence, healing" (n = 8), "Awareness of Exodus ministries, financial/spiritual support" (n = 8), "Treat homosexuality like other sins" (n = 6), "Deal with same-sex attraction in the church" (n = 5), "Find out about programs for healing" (n = 4), and "Have healthy heterosexuals develop healthy relationships with strugglers" (n = 2).

The integration of religious or spiritual concerns and sexual identity was apparent from the qualitative answers received from both LGB-identified and dis-identified participants in response to the question, "Some people cope with their experiences of same-sex attraction by connecting it to the 'big picture' about who God is or what life is about. How do you connect your present sexual identity to this 'big picture'?"

Among the LGB-identified participants, several salient themes emerged on the topic of sexuality and spirituality. Forty-five percent stated that they were LGB as part of God's plan: "I think we (queerfolk) fit into God's diverse creation plan. This isn't a way to 'cope' with same-sex attraction. I've always accepted my orientation. It is an observation about the wonderful diversity in human sexuality." Twenty percent of LGB-identified respondents stated that God loves them just as they are. For example, 1 participant stated, "I believe in a loving God who doesn't judge me for being gay. I'm put on earth to love people and that's what's important." God does not make mistakes or "junk" was reported by 10%, and another 10% stated that their relationship with God is greater than their sexuality: "Actually, as I have matured in my faith, I have come to believe that God really is not interested in my sexuality. God is more concerned about my communication with Him and my relationships with those around me." One LGB-identified individual admitted that the "big picture" was not a concern,

> I guess I don't get the "big picture" because I've never questioned who
> I am. And I never thought God would not accept me because of my

sexuality. My worry through life was how could I get the rest of the
world to accept me, so I've lived a fairly lonely life until recently.

As expected, members of the dis-identified group elucidated different
themes from those reported by the LGB-identified group. Twenty-one
percent reported that they were created for intimacy with God,

> My "big picture" tells me that God created me first for relationship
> with Himself and that I must first seek to satisfy the desire to know and
> be known in Him. Otherwise, all other relationships will be empty or
> counter productive. As I delight myself in Him, then He will bring
> good people into my life.

Twenty-nine percent of dis-identified participants claimed that they were
created for a heterosexual relationship by God, "I feel like healthy heterosexuality is the perfect reflection of the image of God" and "My
present sexual identity is connected to what God has designed me to be—
a woman, a heterosexual woman." God's purpose for living was reported as the integration of their sexuality and spirituality for 11.7%, as
elucidated by one individual, "I feel that life holds no purpose if we are
not serving God. If we choose to live outside His will, then we reject
Him and forfeit both the true satisfaction in this life, and eternal life."
Likewise, the same percentage were in the process of growing into the
person God created them to be, "I struggle with same-sex attraction
because of sin in my life and choices I have made. The 'big picture' is a
process or journey I am on to return back to the me God created me to
be." God's power for change was also reported by 11.7% of the dis-
identified group. 8.8% reported that they were identified in Christ, and
the same percentage said they were created in God's image, "I believe
that God created me in His image and that He has created us as male or
female—in general I believe to stray from this design is sin and very
destructive." Two respondents realized they had projected their relationship struggles with others onto God. One of these participants stated,

> Just as I felt disconnected to males, thinking they were insensitive,
> unable to relate to females, I saw God in the same way in my life. I still
> have a hard time truly believing that God loves, and that God is mer-
> ciful and just when relating to me.

Thus, it appears that for participants in both the LGB-identified and dis-identified groups who experience same-sex attraction, spirituality is often connected with and is intrinsic to their sexuality. The notion of "creation" undergirded themes in both groups and pertained to the resolution of feelings of incongruence regarding sexuality and spirituality in each.

While analyzing the data for the pilot study, we realized that we required objective measures of religiosity, since we wondered if both LGB-identified and dis-identified participants experienced their faith similarly. Thus, for the sexual identity project, two assessments were administered: the Religious Commitment Inventory (RCI-10) and the Intrinsic Religiosity Measurement Scale (IRMS). We considered that "ceiling" effects would be elicited because both groups might endorse items indicating a high commitment to their faith, in addition to identifying faith as an intrinsic motivator in their lives. Yet, despite this concern, both measures were included. The RCI-10 is a ten-item Likert-scaled evaluation in which participants rate religious commitment, as defined by attitudes and behaviors which reinforce beliefs, values, and practices of religious faith. The IRMS is also a ten-item Likert scale that evaluates intrinsic religious motivation (i.e., the internal versus external motivation) of participants.

On the RCI-10 (see Table 6) a moderately significant difference was found between LGB-identified and dis-identified participants. The LGB-identified participants averaged a score of 40.19 (range = 19-50, SD = 12.19), compared to 44.70 (range = 33-50, SD = 5.14), ($F(1, 51)$ = 3.58, p = .064). Several distinctions in response patterns were noted by the greater endorsement of certain items in each group. On balance, LGB-identified participants provided a greater range of responses to each item compared with the dis-identified group. For example, 55% of LGB-identified participants responded with "totally true of me" to the item "My religious beliefs lie behind my whole approach to life," compared with 70.6% of the dis-identified participants. Likewise, 40% of LGB-identified participants stated that it was "totally true" of them to "spend time growing in understanding of my faith," compared with 67.6% of the dis-identified participants. For 35% of LGB-identified participants, "Religious beliefs influence all my dealings in life" was a "totally true" response, versus 64.7% of dis-identified participants. In response to "Religion is especially important to me because it answers many questions about the meaning of life," 50% of LGB-identified participants responded "totally true" in comparison to 76.5% of dis-identified mem-

Table 6. *A Comparison of Scores on the RCI-10*

RCI-10 Themes	Not true	Somewhat true	Moderately true	Mostly true	Totally true
My religious beliefs lie behind my whole approach to life		5%	10%	30% *29.4%*	55% *70.6%*
I spend time trying to grow in understanding of my faith		5% *2.9%*	15% *5.9%*	40% *20.6%*	40% *67.6%*
It is important to me to spend periods of time in private religious thought and reflection	5%	5%	5% *11.8%*	40% *23.5%*	40% *64.7%*
Religious beliefs influence all my dealings in life		10%	25% *2.9%*	30% *32.4%*	35% *64.7%*
Religion is especially important to me because it answers many questions about the meaning of life	10%	5%	15% *2.9%*	15% *20.6%*	50% *76.5%*
I often read books and magazines about my faith	10%	15%	5% *17.6%*	25% *26.5%*	45% *55.9%*
I enjoy working in the activities of my religious organization		5%	5% *8.8%*	20% *41.2%*	70% *47.1%*
I enjoy spending time with others of my religious affiliation			10% *2.9%*	10% *23.5%*	80% *70.5%*
I keep well informed about my local religious group and have some influence on its decisions	*2.9%*	25% *11.8%*	5% *26.5%*	25% *17.6%*	45% *38.2%*
I make financial contributions to my religious organization			5% *5.9%*	30% *2.9%*	65% *88.2%*

Note: LGB-identified = non-italicized, dis-identified = italicized.

bers. It is worth noting that higher percentages of LGB-identified participants reported that it is "totally true" that they "enjoy[ed] working in the activities of [their] religious organization" (70%) and that they "enjoyed spending time with others of [their] religions affiliation" (80%), compared with dis-identified participants (47.1% and 70.5%, respectively).

Likewise for the IRMS, a statistically significant difference was found between the LGB-identified and dis-identified groups on their average scores (see Table 7). LGB-identified participants averaged 18.70 (range = 10-43, SD = 7.97), compared with dis-identified participants, with a mean score of 11.65 (range = 10-18, SD = 2.45). Hoge's average score was 19.70. Although both LGB-identified and LGB-dis-identified groups were found to be below the mean, the significant difference found between these means reflects a greater propensity for dis-identified participants to self-report intrinsic religious motivation. This is not only evidenced by the differences in means, but also by the larger standard deviation found among the scores of individuals who are LGB-identified. Thus, in terms of their responses to the IRMS, there does appear to be a difference between the groups; however, this difference may be due to what "religion" and "religious motivation" mean to dis-identified and LGB-identified individuals. Put differently, the differences between means seems to be noteworthy, but it does not necessarily mean that dis-identified participants really are more intrinsically motivated, only that they responded as such. Perhaps they identified more readily with the concepts proposed by Hodge, which tends to reflect a more traditional religious perspective than that which may be endorsed by LGB-identified participants.

Beyond looking at means, we can also examine response patterns that varied between the groups, with each endorsing particular items more frequently. For example, with respect to "seek[ing] God's guidance when making every important decision," answers varied in the LGB-identified group, with 10% stating that they "moderately disagreed," 20% "moderately agreeing," and 70% "strongly agreeing," compared with 97% of dis-identified participants, who "strongly agreed" with the statement. A greater proportion of LGB-identified group members "strongly agreed" (90%) that they "experienced the presence of the Divine" in their lives, compared with 73.5% of dis-identified participants. 30% of LGB-identified participants "strongly disagree" that their "faith sometimes restricts [their] actions," whereas 79.4% of the dis-identified group "strongly agree" to the same item. Fifty-five percent of LGB-

Table 7. A Comparison of Scores on the IRMS

IRMS Themes	Strongly disagree	Moderately disagree	Moderately agree	Strongly agree
My faith involves all my life	5%		20% *14.7%*	75% *85.3%*
One should seek God's guidance when making every important decision		10%	20% *2.9%*	70% *97%*
In my life I experience the presence of the Divine		5% *2.9%*	5% *20.6%*	90% *73.5%*
My faith sometimes restricts my actions	30%	25%	35% *17.6%*	10% *79.4%*
Nothing is as important to me as serving God as best I know how	5%	10% *2.9%*	25% *14.7%*	60% *82.3%*
I try hard to carry my religion over into all my other dealings in life		15%	30% *11.8%*	55% *88.2%*
My religious beliefs are what really lie behind my whole approach to life	10%	5%	20% *11.8%*	65% *88.2%*
It doesn't matter so much what I believe so long as I lead a moral life	35% *79.4%*	45% *20.6%*		20%
Although I am a religious person, I refuse to let religious considerations influence my everyday affairs	45% *94.1%*	40% *2.9%*	10%	5%
Although I believe in my religion, I feel there are many more important things in life	45% *82.4%*	40% *11.8%*	15% *5.9%*	

Note: LGB-identified = non-italicized, dis-identified = italicized.

identified participants, compared with 88.2% of dis-identified participants "strongly agree" that they "try hard to carry [their] religion over
into all [their] other dealings in life." Similar proportions were reported
for the item, "My religious beliefs are what really lie behind my whole
approach to life," with 65% of LGB-identified participants who "strongly
agree" compared with 88.2% of the dis-identified group. A greater proportion of LGB-identified participants gave higher scores to items measuring extrinsic motivation. For example, 35% of LGB-identified group
members "strongly disagree" to the statement, "It doesn't matter so much
what I believe so long as I lead a moral life," compared with 79.4% of
dis-identified participants. Moreover, 20% of LGB-identified participants
"strongly agree" with that statement. Forty-five percent of LGB-identified participants "strongly disagree" with the statement, "Although I
am a religious person, I refuse to let religious considerations influence
my everyday affairs," compared with 94.1% of dis-identified participants. Likewise, the statement, "Although I believe in my religion, I feel
there are many more important things in life," was scored as "strongly
disagree" by 45% of LGB-identified participants, compared with 82.4%
of dis-identified group members.

Discussion of Themes and Psychological Processes

As we reflect on the themes and psychological processes associated with
sexual identity synthesis, we provide Figure 1 as a visual depiction of the
following themes: age of identity synthesis, emotional reactions, experiences that constrained and facilitated sexual identity synthesis, and feelings associated with synthesis.

Age at Time of Initial Attribution or Identity Synthesis?

It is interesting to compare these findings with the extant research on
sexual identity development. The general thinking in the sexual identity
literature is that labelling as "gay" occurs between the ages of 15-18
years. This is believed to occur, on average, about two years prior to
first disclosure.[19] However, our sample was older at the time of self-
report of sexual identity synthesis. The generic timeline for LGB labelling may more accurately refer to initial attribution rather than final identity synthesis. Moreover, perhaps by focusing on religiously-affiliated
individuals, we have introduced a variable that complicates labeling at a

younger age because conflictual feelings of same-sex attraction and religious values have to be integrated.

Emotional Reactions

Both LGB-identified and dis-identified participants reported various emotions due to uncertainty about same-sex attraction and identification. Fear
was among the most common emotion of both groups. Half of the LGB-
identified respondents reported fear, as did one-third of those who dis-
identified with an LGB-identity. For both groups of participants, it appears that fear stemmed from uncertainty about the outcome of
LGB-identification or dis-identification. Over time, and with focus on
their process of dis-identification, fewer dis-identified respondents were
fearful. This coincides with the increased number of dis-identified participants who presently feel joy and peace, compared with the proportion
who reported those same feelings upon initial dis-identification.

Experiences That Constrain and Facilitate Identity Synthesis

The constraints to one's current sexual identity synthesis suggest remarkably different experiences. The LGB group focused more on society and
possible reactions from family members and the church. The dis-identified group pointed to having various needs (emotional, physical) met as
the chief constraint. Certainly the cost was high for both groups as they
persevered toward sexual identity synthesis.

Among those who identified LGB, the same-sex attraction itself facilitated a sexual identity synthesis. Social contacts were also important,
and this coincides with the extant literature on sexual identity development and the "coming out" process.[20] In contrast, for those who dis-
identified, God and the conviction of the Holy Spirit were important in
facilitating their sexual identity synthesis. Although more than half also
reported that same-sex relationships were unfulfilling and functioned as
a sort of disincentive, an experience with transcendent or supernatural
reality appears to be a key aspect of attribution and meaning-making.
This theme was further elaborated when those who dis-identified stated
that their religious/spiritual worldview, expressed through prayer and
worship, was a resource for coping.

This raises the question of the influence of religion and spirituality
during the attainment of sexual identity synthesis. We turn now to a

Figure 1. *Themes Characteristic of Sexual Identity Synthesis*

Age at Identity Synthesis	Constraints	Facilitating Influences	Feelings at Synthesis
LGB-Identified	Stigma (80%)	Same-sex attraction (80%)	Self-acceptance (75%)
~26 years old	Fear/not hurt family (60%)	LGB community (80%)	Relief (65%)
	Spiritual cost (50%)	Intimate relationship (60%)	Peace (65%)
	Neg. family relationships (50%)	Same-sex behavior (55%)	
LGB-Dis-Identified	Emotional needs (47%)	God's intervention (88%)	Relief (44%)
~34 years old	Lifestyle (47%)	Conviction/Holy Spirit (77%)	Peace (35%)
	Ambivalence (32%)	Support groups (65%)	Sadness (32%)
		Unhappy in lifestyle (59%)	Fear (32%)

discussion of what happens when religious ideology and commitments and same-sex attraction intersect. We begin with an initial discussion of interesting findings from an ethnographic study of the same population.

When Religion and Same-Sex Attractions Intersect

Based on data from her ethnographic study of UFMCC and Exodus participants, Wolkomir[21] reports on the "ideological maneuvering that enabled" UFMCC members "to claim the authority to revise Christian ideology." According to Wolkomir, the process involved deconstructing existing ideology that condemns same-sex behavior, developing a new and LGB-affirming ideology, and "authenticating new self-meanings."[22] As she suggests, both UFMCC and Exodus members tend to commit themselves to Christianity and meanwhile sort through the complex choices associated with their same-sex attraction.

What we found that is similar to Wolkomir's report is that participants realized that their same-sex attraction was a more enduring aspect of their sexual identity, and that this realization can lead to a subjective feeling of alienation from their Christian faith. The alienation can be felt both ideologically (or theologically, in terms of the moral status of same-sex behavior), and also practically, as they often fear rejection from family and friends, who presumably share their religion. According to Wolkomir,

> Resolving their dilemma required that the men do revisionist ideological work to alter the meaning of the identity "Christian," in accord with their respective group's definition as well as to accommodate their sexual desires and behaviors in ways that felt legitimate.[23]

Rather than take on Scripture as their source of truth, the men in Wolkomir's study tended to challenge what they viewed as "human faults" in the interpretation of the Bible. UFMCC members rejected traditional interpretation condemning same-sex behavior, and Exodus members "recast homosexual struggle as righteousness."[24]

Both groups constructed an affirming ideology. The LGB-affirming group "applied secularized notions of social justice to their situations,"[25] focusing on greater inclusivity and the notion that God loves everyone. In contrast, the ex-gay group (or what we refer to as the LGB-dis-identifying group) focused more on the "fallen human" condition. They emphasized the claim that all people sin, including parents. They held that "homosexuality resulted from emotional trauma created by the sins of other (and important) people in their early lives," perceiving that same-sex attraction was "a result of unmet psychological or emotional needs becoming sexualized."[26]

Following these two outlined paths, those who affirmed their LGB identity saw themselves as tolerant and inclusive of others, while those who rejected an LGB identity viewed themselves as "righteous strugglers."[27] These are certainly intriguing and distinct paths, and they appear to lead to yet another important distinction: between authenticity and idolatry.

We can distinguish between a concern for authenticity among those who identified with an LGB sexual identity, and a concern about idolatry among those who dis-identified with an LGB identity synthesis. A number of LGB identified participants seemed to be communicating a concern for personal authenticity. They refused to deny who they "really are," and attempts to deny or minimize their same-sex attraction—and eventually their personal identity as LGB—evolved to the point of inauthenticity. "Coming out" felt synonymous with a healthy sexual identity synthesis, as it was a means to congruence between their internal feelings and their external lives.

Conversely, those who dis-identified with an LGB identity seemed more concerned about idolatry. Richard Lints[28] discusses the relationship between idolatry and the image of God, and his analysis seems to comply with the themes of those who dis-identified. From a traditional Christian perspective, idolatry, if distilled in its purest form, is actually about subverting one's relationship with God. Individuals who dis-identified with an LGB identity were committed to *not* integrating their same-sex attraction into an LGB identity; for those participants, making the self-defining attribution, "I am gay," seemed incongruent with their identity and emphasized certain aspects of identity to which they were unwilling to commit. Put differently, those who dis-identified with an LGB identity chose not choose to privilege their identity as LGB and relate to God on those terms.

The aforementioned explanation is consistent with our findings. We report statistically significant differences between the LGB-identified and dis-identified participants on measures of religious commitment and intrinsic/extrinsic religiosity. As mentioned in Chapter 3, religious commitment refers to "the degree to which a person adheres to his or her religious values, beliefs, and practices and employs them in daily living."[29] Dis-identified individuals tended to score higher on this measure, suggesting the likelihood of a high commitment to religious values and life in accordance with a religious explanatory framework.

Similarly, those who dis-identified usually scored higher on intrinsic religiosity, which corresponds to adherence to religious belief "on faith" (rather than ulterior motive). Though it should be noted that both groups on average scored above one standard deviation, suggesting that both groups are intrinsically religious. The relative elevations on both measures (among those who dis-identify) may make sense, given that those who dis-identify with an LGB identity are committed to a path consistent with Christian pronouncements on the moral status of same-sex behavior. This factor emerges, despite undergoing contradictory thought processes in order to "level the playing field" among sins, so that same-sex attraction and behavior is regarded as no worse than other sins in a "fallen" world. In contrast, LGB-identified participants may be undergoing a more profound "ideological transformation," to use Wolkomir's language. These individuals may be willing to modify religious beliefs and values in order to be consistent with one's choices in life, particularly if behavior is an expression of commitment to an LGB sexual identity.

Part 3

Implications for Theory, Research and Practice

Chapter 7

Theory, Research and Practice

Introduction

In an attempt to understand at face value the experiences of those who identify and dis-identify with a lesbian, gay, or bisexual (LGB) identity, we have organized findings from the pilot study and larger survey comprising *dilemma, development*, and *synthesis*. As discussed previously, the dilemma refers to the objective reality in which a person experiences same-sex attraction in a predominantly heterosexual society and within the context of Christian faith and/or upbringing. For want of a better word, the signified "endpoint" is known as identity synthesis. The path one navigates from dilemma to synthesis is known as sexual identity development. By organizing data around three broad areas of experience, we attain our basic conceptual framework, which allows us to comprehend the data and record the stories of participants. We attend now to the implications of these findings for mental health professionals, which will be discussed under the headings *theory, research*, and *clinical practice*.

In the first section, theory, we highlight the value of diversity by encouraging theorists to be more inclusive of others with whom they are unfamiliar, and to avoid pathologizing individuals who dis-identify with same-sex attraction. We also suggest the need for clarity about what it means to dis-identify with an LGB-identity synthesis. Finally, we suggest that a concerted effort be made to link theories of sexual identity development to the stress and coping literature and to consider whether identity synthesis is more fluid than commonly supposed.

Theory

Becoming More Inclusive

The most salient implication of this study is the question of whether theorists are sufficiently inclusive in their theorizing about sexual identity development. When framing theories around the development of an LGB identity synthesis tacit assumptions are made about those who dis-identify with an LGB identity. We recognize that, on occasion, theorists have considered "LGB-dis-identified" individuals, but many efforts to include these voices have failed to reach a full and sympathetic engagement. The tendency for many theorists has been to pathologize them or assume a level of arrested development because they have not yet achieved an LGB identity synthesis. For example, in their review of the extant literature, McCarn and Fassinger[1] observe that,

> individuals may be in several stages of development simultaneously, not all individuals will negotiate all stages, and the process of moving from early awareness to identity integration is a lengthy one . . . linear models tend to ignore the paths of those who do not progress predictably through the stages or to view alternative outcomes (bisexuality, heterosexuality) as developmental arrest.

We encourage theorists to avoid pathologizing those who dis-identify with an LGB identity synthesis. A tendency to stigmatize those who dis-identify with an LGB identity is also evident in theories and research on sexual identity and in clinical practice. For example, in a chapter on working with sexual minorities, Nichols[2] offers an account of her treatment team's response to "Herb," who was reporting confusion about his sexual identity. He is described as having had same-sex fantasies but no experience, and was "not entirely sure" he was "heterosexual" but "couldn't imagine being gay." Nonetheless, the treatment team concluded that his case was "highly unusual." "Therefore" they "considered Herb's struggle with sexual identity symptomatic of a deeper, entrenched problem and diagnosed him with avoidant personality disorder."[3] Perhaps additional information was available to the treatment team than was reported in the case vignette, but what was reported is troubling; it suggests that the confusion and potential conflict with an LGB identity is itself a symptom of pathology, in this case a longstanding, chronic characterological problem.

Similarly, in his discussion of sexual identity development, Troiden discusses those who choose to live a chaste life, who have decided not to act on their feelings of same-sex attraction:

> Women and men who capitulate avoid homosexual activity because they have internalized a stigmatizing view of homosexuality. The persistence of homosexual feelings in the absence of homosexual activity, however, may lead them to experience self-hatred and despair.[4]

This characterization of those who choose to dis-identify with an LGB identity through (at least) refraining from same-sex behavior is offered without empirical support, and again seems biased against those who dis-identify with an LGB-ideology.

We would like to see greater respect for and increased efforts towards understanding those who dis-identify with an LGB identity, or who are, at minimum, weighing aspects of their identity, which they may choose to privilege over other aspects. This would seem to be an improvement over treating "the other side" as anomalous. Barash,[5] in his discussion of anomalies in psychology, admits that ". . . a disease syndrome is by definition an anomaly (with normal being the default condition), and once again, anomalies tend to be ignored unless and until they can be retro-recognized within a grander interpretive framework." There appears to be the need for an explanatory model that removes those who dis-identify out of the category of anomaly and into the category of normality, as one possible outcome among those who experience same-sex attraction.

Need for Clarity in Identity

There does not appear to be a name that accurately captures the experience of those we refer to as "dis-identifying" with an LGB-identity synthesis. Is it sufficient for theorists to conceptualize an identity synthesis as a possible outcome with respect to the "opposite" of an LGB identity synthesis? Is "dis"-identification really a veritable sense of one's sexual identity?

We recognize that one of the challenges in answering this question is to consider alternatives. For example, one could argue that the people who "dis-identify" with an LGB identity synthesis are simply identifying with a heterosexual identity, and have actually achieved a heterosexual identity synthesis. After all, when offered a choice among various labels (i.e., heterosexual, bisexual, homosexual), the majority of dis-identified participants in our studies self-identified as heterosexual.

The problem with this assumption, in our view, is first that it conflates private and public identity and assumes a zero-sum experience with sexual identity at the outset. A person may dis-identify and so may be presumed by others to be heterosexual, and the person may also have a public identity as heterosexual. However, this says precious little about the person's private identity. What an individual presents may be in sharp contrast and in potential conflict with who that individual actually is. A lack of congruence may instigate various personal, relational, emotional, or functional difficulties. Consequently, uninformed assumptions may reinforce negative affectual experiences expressed in an individual's state of conflict.

Our second concern is the assumption that, not being LGB, the person is therefore categorically heterosexual. Clinical experience suggests that some people who shift from an LGB identity may experience a decrease in the intensity of same-sex attraction that is not met with an automatic increase in opposite sex attraction. The result is that some people report asexuality for a period of time; this eludes theorists who pursue the language of a "heterosexual identity synthesis" as the counterpoint to an LGB identity synthesis. Without succinct descriptions of experience, we risk categorizing individuals according to our biases and presuppositions.[6]

Political Dimensions of Sexual Identity

Many of the discussions surrounding sexual identity seem to have political implications. Generally speaking, we encourage theorists and researchers to avoid politicizing this type of work. However, we recognize that certain concepts may shed more light on our understanding of sexual identity.

For example, Roger Smith,[7] in his discussion of political theory and identity, provides us with a concept that may prove useful in analyses and discussions of the political dynamics of sexual identity. He distinguishes between ethnic and civic views of ethical stories and political identity. An ethnic political identity refers to unchosen aspects of identity. In contrast, a civic view of identity is one "in which membership rests on voluntary agreement as to political procedures and principles."[8]

Through a variety of means, these ethnic and civic components of identity are ultimately tied to ethically constitutive stories. Smith defines ethically constitutive stories as "an account explaining why membership in a political community is intrinsic to who its members truly are."[9] It should be increasingly clear that both outcomes we have studied—having an LGB identity or dis-identifying with an LGB identity—are ethically constitutive stories of sorts. Although stakeholders more familiar with a specific identity outcome may disagree with whether their identity synthesis is intrinsically political, both rely upon an explanatory framework that points to aspects of authenticity within individuals.

We would also note that both explanatory frameworks draw upon facets of both ethnic and civic identity. There are certainly "givens" associated with an LGB identity, namely, the fact that the individuals experience same-sex attraction. Yet there are also civic dimensions to an LGB sexual identity. The decision to integrate one's experience of same-sex attraction into an LGB identity synthesis is an act of civic identification to the extent that one voluntarily agrees with an LGB explanatory framework, including the people and organizations which affirm that explanatory framework. The same appears to be true for those who dis-identify with an LGB identity. Again, the ethnic dimension is the experience of same-sex attraction. None of those who dis-identified ever *chose* to experience same-sex attraction; the reaction of same-sex attraction was entirely involuntary. The civic dimension comprises what the individual chooses to do with the attractions he or she has. This civic dimension is again reflected in one's attributions and explanatory framework, as these shape sexual identity over time. Again, we urge our colleagues to avoid politicizing the work undertaken in the area of sexual identity development. However, certain political dimensions may aid our understanding of key concepts. These have not been explored sufficiently, and we believe various constructs may prove promising if developed further.

Connections with the Coping Literature

In Chapter 6 we introduced a possible tie into the coping literature. This is an area for future consideration, as theories of coping appear to be a promising fit for how both LGB-identified and dis-identified individuals respond to same-sex attraction. We predict that this language will have greater appeal to those who dis-identify with an LGB-identity synthesis because they can conceptualize their experience as coping with same-sex attraction as well as coping with messages received from LGB-affirming ideologies and the people and communities supporting that identity. Although those who identify with an LGB identity synthesis may concede to an element of coping involved when in a dilemma or when feeling negative emotions, such as confusion or tension, they would not want their coping to be confused with the notion that they are entering a "moratorium" regarding an LGB identity, per se. After all, most LGB-identified participants in our study did not re-appraise their decision to identify as LGB.

So we acknowledge the likelihood of disagreement among theorists about the advantages of considering the stress and coping literature. But we emphasize coping with the experience of same-sex attraction in light of both a predominantly heterosexual society and a Christian ideological framework, which has historically considered engagement in same-sex behavior as immoral. Among the many models of stress and coping, we consider and apply our findings to the meaning-making model of Park and Folkman,[10] who observe pathways that involve stress, coping, and meaning-making. In their model, upon experiencing a stressful event, the individual makes initial attributions and appraises the meaning of attributions with reference to both *situational* meaning (present circumstances) and *global* meaning (beliefs and expectations about God, the world, order, and so on). If experience and situational meaning are congruent, stress does not occur. If incongruent, the individual will undergo a period of coping with the stressful situation, and may employ a number of specific strategies, including attempts to transform the global meanings attached to their circumstances.

In the case of those who identify or dis-identify with an LGB affirming ideology, the actual experience of attraction (in their sociocultural context) is the initial stressor. As a person realizes feelings of same-sex attraction, they make initial attributions and come to appraise the meaning of the attributions in relation to both situational meaning (attraction in the here-and-now) and their global meaning (in this case, a Christian explanatory framework). If experience and related situational meaning are congruent with global meaning, stress is not an issue and essentially, the individual integrates same-sex attraction into an LGB identity synthesis in line with many of the existing models of LGB identity synthesis.

If, however, there is stress, as suggested by this study and others,[11] the individual turns to various coping activities, such as emotion-focused and problem-focused coping activities. Among identified individuals, activities might include social support and time spent with like-minded others, establishment of same-sex intimate relationships, reading of literature, identifying with the attraction (saying to oneself, "My attraction signals who I 'really am'"), and so on. In contrast, dis-identified individuals might turn to like-minded others, dis-identify with an LGB identity (telling oneself, for example, "My attractions signal an 'unmet need'"). The person also considers an ideological transformation of the global meaning found in a traditional Christian explanatory framework with reference to interpretations of an LGB identity and same-sex behavior. It is in this sense that the Metropolitan Community Church seems to provide a transformed Christian ideological framework that supports an LGB identity synthesis.

The issue of stigma should not be downplayed and the impact of being "different" in a negative way can be profound. Presumably, most people will fail to identify with something they see as bad. If one's beliefs and values conflict with same-sex attraction and behavior, what happens next? Some individuals may reframe their attitude of same-sex attraction as more positive and in accord with an LGB-affirming ideology. Others face the dilemma and require congruence between current situation (feeling same-sex attraction) and the meanings attached to that—and global meaning (with respect to their view of God and the world). In considering either of these broad life trajectories, then, if coping activities and ideological transformation lead to congruence, individuals reach a consolidated sexual identity. If not, they *revisit* coping activities and the global meaning associated with beliefs and values about the world, God, and human sexuality, identity and behavior. Again, same-sex attraction is a potential stressor in a predominantly heterosexual society, and the conceptualization of same-sex attraction as a stressor is at least a starting point for the application of models of coping and meaning-making. A number of new developments may arise in our understanding of sexual identity development and synthesis as theorists analyze the linkages between sexual identity theory and the stress and coping literature.

Is "Synthesis" an Endpoint?

In part because we raise the question of re-consideration of sexual identity, we have to ask whether "identity synthesis" is properly conceptualized as an endpoint. By doing so, theorists assume a somewhat linear model with a starting point and an endpoint, but little room remains for the kind of sexual flexibility evidenced in some studies, particularly of lesbian identity synthesis.

Also, can we say with certainty that the participants in our study have achieved "synthesis"? They certainly report feeling as if they have attained identity congruence. Might some participants reconsider their identity at a later point in time and pursue another identity? The design of our analysis does not allow for the answer to these questions, nor do we assume that synthesis is the definitive endpoint due to design limitations.

This brings us to a natural transition to the implications for research. Just as there are a number of important implications for theorists, there are several issues we would raise for consideration among researchers.

Research

Although some of the early models of sexual identity theory are grounded more firmly in theory than empirical research, we see today a concerted effort to combine theory and research. As we reflect on the implications of our study, we first mention the implication of the stories of those who dis-identified with an LGB-identity synthesis, as well as the potential value of collaboration among researchers who have access to these populations. Research is the domain in which we operationalize various constructs, including that of "dis-identification." As mentioned above, this construct requires further analysis. Also, because we view the coping literature as a promising approach to the study of this population, we encourage an intentional tie between coping literature and the research on sexual identity development and synthesis. Finally, we encourage research design that can allow us to monitor over time individuals who achieve synthesis; that way we can better understand if identity synthesis is indeed an endpoint.

Include Participants Who Represent the Entire Population

There is an apparent need to establish studies that draw from both populations—those who have achieved an LGB identity synthesis and those who have dis-identified with an LGB identity. By doing so researchers in psychology refer to the etic/emic distinction from anthropology. According to Dalton, Elias, and Wandersman:

Cross-cultural psychology takes an etic perspective, which compares cultures in universal terms. . . . In an emic study, researchers see to understand one culture "from the inside," in its own terms, with as little reference to other cultures' concepts as possible.[12]

To adopt a truly emic perspective, researchers could conceptualize either two distinct populations—those who identify and those who dis-identify with an LGB identity—or one population of those who experience same-sex attraction. We prefer the latter approach because it is broader and more descriptive with fewer a priori assumptions. If the latter tactic is chosen, researchers might identify the one population as individuals who experience same-sex attraction, and then draw on a sample more representative of that population. Although we see benefits to in-depth separate studies of those who identify and those who dis-identify, we think it more accurate and helpful to conceptualize one population rather than two. By studying primarily those who achieve an LGB synthesis, there is the possibility of overlooking or ignoring the anomalous individuals as they gradually attain an alternative identity synthesis. In a worst case scenario, there is the risk that researchers will pathologize individuals who dis-identify with an LGB identity.

Collaboration among Researchers

We mentioned above that research on sexual identity development and synthesis may benefit from concerted efforts at collaboration among researchers who conceptualize these issues differently and who have access to different populations. One reason is that although clinical and research informed information about a particular population may be readily available, an experiential understanding of and empathy towards a particular group (e.g., dis-identified individuals) may facilitate increased accuracy and depth of study. More importantly, collaboration enables researchers to de-mystify the experiences of those whose stories are relatively unknown.[13]

With respect to access, we think it particularly difficult to engage with the populations discussed in the Sexual Identity Project. Wolkomir[14] mentions in the report on her ethnographic study that she had encountered barriers to access to both UFMCC and Exodus, and that Exodus was much more reticent and wary than the UFMCC group.

With regard to ease of access and collaboration, researchers who approach sexual identity issues with specific explanatory frameworks may be striving to accurately represent the sexual minorities with whom they are most familiar. Unfortunately, by doing so, they may also use a hermeneutic or interpretive framework, which potentially neglects or overlooks the studies and explanatory frameworks of other researchers.

Operationalize a Positive Alternative Identity

In part because there has been scant research on those who dis-identify with their same-sex attraction, little has been done to operationalize a positive alternative identity. When we discuss an LGB identity, there is apparently greater consensus about what we mean, although there may be greater in-group diversity than assumed. Only through our understanding of the LGB community will we increasingly appreciate the diversity within the community. Likewise, our understanding of those who dis-identify will be furthered as we conduct research that includes them. We anticipate diversity within this community as well, and perhaps recognition of that diversity will lead researchers to better constructs able to capture experiences of individuals who pursue an alternative (to an LGB) sexual identity synthesis.

As mentioned earlier, an obvious (but simplistic) response has been to operationalize as heterosexual those who dis-identify with an LGB identity. However, our concern is that this presumption falls into distinct essentialist categories, which may fail to fully reflect the experiences of those who dis-identify, this being due to assumptions that do not take into consideration the various and complex dimensions of sexual identity. Such important questions should be studied empirically.

Test Coping Theories with This Population

We think the opportunity now exists for researchers to apply and test theories of coping within this population. This might reveal a more constructive avenue for studying the wider population of individuals who experience same-sex attraction, and it might help researchers avoid the tendency to pathologize either those who identify or those who dis-identify with an LGB affirming ideology.

We mentioned the model of stress and coping by Park and Folkman, and several other models may be worth exploring empirically. We do not deny the potential political ramifications of this type of study, as coping is probably best conceptualized as coping with an objective dilemma (of same-sex attraction in a largely heterosexual society couched in a Christian explanatory framework) and not merely as an LGB identity as such. Scientists can gain increased knowledge of these issues, and can contribute to a common understanding through the shared language of empirical research.

Track Those in "Synthesis" over Time

An additional research consideration is the benefit of monitoring over time those who claim to have achieved an identity synthesis. Whether they are LGB-identified or dis-identified, it would seem logical to set up a longitudinal study designed to determine the extent to which individuals' identity synthesis is an endpoint. Given the existing findings on lesbian and bisexual identity development alone, this kind of research design seems warranted.

For example, in Diamond's[15] study of 89 young women who self-identified as lesbian or bisexual, the mean age was 20 years (SD = 1.95), and our study suggests that an older sample or wider age range may help us widen our understanding of sexual identity development and synthesis. It is possible too that synthesis is an artificial endpoint, and that some percentage of people undergo sexual identity "chapters" based on factors that could be studied empirically.

Clinical Practice

As we turn to our final major area of focus, clinical practice, we will discuss the implications of recognizing multiple stakeholders in therapy, as well as the importance of an emic perspective towards people from unfamiliar cultural or religious backgrounds. We also discuss a continuum of services and the role of existing resources, as well as coping in the context of sexual identity development.

Recognize Multiple Stakeholders

There are multiple stakeholders in discussions of sexual identity. By discussing how sexual identity develops and reaches synthesis over time, we are necessarily discussing a timeframe ranging from childhood (around 8-10 years old) to late adolescence and young adulthood (ages 28-35). Across this time-span, numerous stakeholders appear, including parents, siblings, teachers, youth leaders, religious leaders (e.g., pastors, ministers, rabbis), neighbors, kinship networks, friends, roommates, and lovers and spouses.[16]

Our starting point is to take an emic approach. We suggested that this perspective is important when designing studies of a population that experiences same-sex attraction. As we turn our attention to clinical service delivery, it is crucial to understand from within a community that community's views of same-sex attraction, sexual identity, and sexual behavior. At the very least this involves empathy with clients. If the individual is identifying as LGB, it is incumbent upon the clinician to see the world through those eyes. The clinician will therefore want to benefit from existing resources that support an LGB identity synthesis.[17]

Likewise, if an individual is dis-identifying with an LGB identity synthesis, taking an emic perspective may facilitate the clinician's understanding of factors pointing to that dis-identification. Is it religious beliefs and values? If so, can the clinician dignify those beliefs and values, even if the she or he does not share them? Again, empathy is necessary in order to assist those with specific beliefs about sexuality, sexual identity, and sexual behavior. Are these beliefs informed by theology? Are there disagreements among those who hold to this religion? What is the basis of those disagreements? What resources are available from that religion to those who adhere to different views?

Routinely assessing religious functioning may be a useful start. Participants in our study shared a religious affiliation, and we think good provision of clinical services would include assessment of religious functioning. Does the potential conflict between same-sex attraction and an LGB identity impact religious functioning? Is this a worthwhile starting point in providing clinical services?

A Continuum of Services

One of the existing debates surrounding sexual identity is whether reorientation therapy is effective. The extreme views of this debate are often underscored, as reorientation therapy is contrasted with gay-integrative treatment; the effect may be to simply polarize the issues into a two "sided" debate rather than help facilitate a collaborative partnership with the goal to provide the best clinical service to each client.

Researchers have suggested the utility of considering a continuum of services for those who experience same-sex attraction.[18] At the very least, this would include adding to gay-integrative treatment and reorientation therapy approaches such as sexual behavior management (or celibacy- or chastity-based approaches) and sexual identity management. The latter approach is particularly interesting in light of our study. How can clinicians help those who identify and those who dis-identify with an LGB identity towards sexual identity synthesis? Might there be an attractive alternative for those not wishing to pursue sexual reorientation therapy, or those dissatisfied with the outcome of their reorientation therapy? Or more precisely, what does it mean to facilitate sexual identity synthesis? Although many of the models of gay-integrative treatment might be viewed as facilitating an LGB identity synthesis, there are few alternatives to reorientation therapy that focus on facilitating an alternative (to an LGB identity) identity synthesis.[19]

Existing Resources

To acknowledge and benefit from existing resources related to those who identify as LGB is significant. For example, the American Psychological Association's (APA) Council of Representatives adopted a resolution for clinicians on Appropriate Therapeutic Responses to Sexual Orientation.[20] Recommendations include anti-discriminatory practices and the removal of the stigma associated with an LGB identity. The resolution also encourages clinicians to distribute accurate information and seek training and consultation, as well as make referrals, as needed.

Another relevant resource is the Division 44 (Society for the Psychological Study of Gay, Lesbian, and Bisexual Issues) document, Guidelines for Psychotherapy with LGB Clients.[21] As in the APA resolution, clinicians are reminded that homosexuality is not a mental illness; furthermore, they should recognize the ways in which society stigmatizes those who identify as LGB, as well as how one's own attitudes and knowledge gaps may limit effective treatment for those who identify as LGB.

Following the publication of the APA Resolution and the Division 44 Guidelines, Schneider, Brown and Glassgold[22] published an article to guide clinicians keen to incorporate the APA Resolution into their practice. The authors provide a number of clinical vignettes to assist clinicians who want to address relevant issues, including for example, possible responses to sexual identity confusion and requests to change sexual orientation.

The above-mentioned resources are potentially valuable to mental health professionals, but they are incomplete, according to some professionals. Although these resources fit the specific framework of LGB-identified individuals and can be tremendously valuable for service delivery from that perspective, dis-identified individuals are rarely discussed in a full and sympathetic manner in these documents. They may find fewer professional resources to meet their needs. Therefore, clinicians who wish to conceptualize a continuum of services will benefit from materials that help navigate sexual identity development and synthesis among those who dis-identify with an LGB identity synthesis.

Coping in the Context of Identity Development

We have suggested that the coping literature may provide a resource for theory and research on sexual identity development and synthesis. The coping literature is also an obvious connection for clinical practice. We hesitate to use the word "coping" due to it potentially being misinterpreted as derogatory about same-sex attraction. However, we use it because it was a repeated theme of a number of participants in our studies. No alternatives to "coping" were suggested. We think one way to bring this literature together is to place clinical issues in the context of the broad framework of *Identity Dilemma*, *Identity Development*, and *Identity Synthesis*.

Identity Dilemma

The first experience is that of the dilemma individuals face when they experience same-sex attraction. This time is often characterized by confusion and tension, and clinical interventions will aim to support the young person, help to build self-esteem, and capitalize on any characteristics of resilience. Other interventions will focus on the importance of social support. Social support can manifest through family and peer group relationships, as well as one's faith community.

A starting point is to comprehend sexual identity concerns within the broader context of development, to reflect on a young person's experience with *identity versus role confusion*, as Erikson would conceptualize it. The key element here is to define the parameters of best practice when working with adolescents and young adults who experience sexual identity confusion, who are trying on various roles in a number of settings and with different people.

Identity Development

When reflecting on identity development it is necessary to identify attributions and relate them to situational meaning and global meaning for the young person. The attributions are how the individual makes sense of same-sex attraction. To what does he or she attribute them? What do they signal, if anything? How are they being understood against the broader backdrop of the young person's beliefs and values about sexuality and sexual behavior?

This time is also appropriate for developing coping skills and social support. For example, Beckstead and Morrow[23] identify variables that seem to facilitate self-acceptance among 50 same-sex attracted individuals within the Church of Jesus Christ of Latter Day Saints (Mormons) who reported feeling conflicted between religious beliefs/values and same-sex attraction. The variables included contact with others who shared their explanatory framework, active participation in a support group, a less negative attitude toward same-sex attraction, clarifying and living by their own ethical and valuative framework, and working toward improved family and peer group relationships. These findings are remarkably similar to those reported by Wolkomir,[24] who discussed the importance of ideological transformation with respect to one's Christian faith and experiences of same-sex attraction, as well as the necessity for validation and social support from others ("emotion work") in groups for those who either identify or dis-identify with an LGB sexual identity.

Let us pause to consider the popular concept of "coming out." The phrase is currently synonymous with public identification of oneself as LGB. However, it may be more helpful to think of "coming out" as limited public acknowledgement of one's experiences of same-sex attraction: limited in that the disclosure may be to close friends, family members, or other key individuals in the person's life, such as a youth minister in one's faith community. To acknowledge same-sex attraction indicates honesty rather than denial or downplaying the attraction due to external pressures. So long as coming out is synonymous with an eventual LGB identity synthesis, the language itself marginalizes those who wish to be open and honest about the objective fact that they experience same-sex attraction (being "out"), but who may choose to dis-identify with an LGB identity synthesis.

Identity Synthesis

It may be helpful to regard synthesis as an endpoint, but to also remain open to the possibility that an individual's current experience of identity synthesis may be one chapter in a larger book of identity. Further research may enlighten us about this experience. However, to date, we do know that individuals look for a "best fit" between beliefs and values and how to choose to live. We call this *congruence*: the reduction or absence of the cognitive dissonance often present among those who experience same-sex attraction, or are moving toward or achieving synthesis.

We found in our study that religion and spirituality are important considerations in our sample insofar as achieving and maintaining identity synthesis are concerned. Those who identified tended to recast Christian theology to accommodate their LGB identity, whereas those who dis-identified tended to change how they thought of their sexual attractions and identity in light of a Christian explanatory framework.

But even this understanding may be too simplistic; it is true that Christian ideological commitments may be changed in order to facilitate synthesis. However, as Wolkomir suggested, ideology can be challenged by both identified and dis-identified individuals. LGB-identified individuals may move toward an ideology of tolerance, utilizing "the biblical precept of 'God loves everyone' to valorize a principle of inclusiveness,"[25] and dis-identified individuals may move toward an ideology of righteousness by elevating "the importance of 'struggling to be righteous' as a Christian precept,"[26] seeing their experience as a calling toward a certain kind of life.

Identity synthesis is undoubtedly assisted by social support with like-minded others. In a separate analysis of ways in which support groups help gay and ex-gay members do "emotion work," Wolkomir[27] discusses how "support group ideologies attach names to dis-eases and write prescriptions for 'curing' them." Regardless of whether groups are LGB affirming, leading to what we call an LGB-identity synthesis, or facilitating dis-identification with an LGB identity and corresponding ideologies, support groups generate sentiments which make "ideological transformation and identity work feel worthwhile."[28]

Conclusion

LGB-identified and LGB-dis-identified individuals share a commonality in addition to the fact that they experience same-sex attraction. To use Smith's language, both an LGB identity and an alternative (to an LGB) identity are "ethically constitutive stories" intended to address the identity of members of a particular subgroup. Interestingly, individuals who report either type of identity synthesis belong to marginalized groups trying to articulate an explanatory framework in which their experience is available to those subscribing to existing, dominant ideologies.

Wolkomir sees both identified and dis-identified groups as "subverting the dominant ideologies that impose stigma," a move required by any marginalized group that wishes to create a new identity.[29] She is quick to note, however, that:

> Although ideological revision provides opportunities for subordinates to challenge dominant ideologies, it is also constrained by and reproduces inequality. Members of subordinate groups are hard-pressed to claim creditable selves, because powerless people, by definition, lack the authority to challenge a dominant ideology. Thus . . . subordinates must find a way to open the interpretive space within which they can deconstruct and suitably revise a key piece of dominant truth before reattaching it to the overarching, legitimating framework.[30]

Unfortunately, these two groups—those who identify and those who dis-identify with an LGB identity—have often found themselves at odds with each other. Those who identify and dis-identify are poised against one another in an ever-expanding political battle for legitimacy and the quest for control of attributions and meaning-making symbols and language. However, there is room for both groups to forge their identities and to meanwhile allow the other to expand cultural meanings. After all, who better to understand and empathize with the experience of the marginalized than those who are also marginalized?

Appendix A

Identity Synthesis Interview

Do you currently see yourself as having

- ☐ **(A) integrated your experiences of same-sex attraction into a lesbian, gay, or bisexual identity, or**
- ☐ **(B) dis-identified or not identified with your experiences of same-sex attraction?**

If they answered "(A)" *please ask the following questions.* If they answered "(B)" *please skip the following questions and begin with the questions on page 157:*

1. Looking back, please comment on whether or not you felt different from others for gender-related reasons, for example, because of your choice of play activities as a child (e.g., trucks vs. dolls, house vs. cops and robbers)?

2. Were you ever confused about your same-sex attraction when most of your peers may not have been experiencing same-sex attraction? Tell me what that was like.

3. What do you think contributed to your questioning your sexual identity?

4. What role, if any, did the following factors play in your attributing your same-sex attractions to a lesbian, gay, or bisexual identity? (Check all that apply):
   ☐ Family (parents, siblings)
   ☐ Peer group
   ☐ Religious community
   ☐ Religious literature (Bible, Torah, Koran, etc.)
   ☐ Gay/Lesbian/Bisexual literature
   Comments:

5. Did you ever attribute your experiences of same-sex attraction to anything other than a possible lesbian, gay, or bisexual identity? If so, please explain:

6. Was there a time when you identified yourself publicly as heterosexual?

7. Was there a time when you identified yourself privately (just to yourself) as heterosexual?

8. Before fully integrating your same-sex attractions into a lesbian, gay, or bisexual identity, what . . .

   (a) hindered this process?

   (b) encouraged this process?

9. Following your initial identification as lesbian, gay, or bisexual, did you ever re-consider your lesbian, gay, or bisexual identity?

10. Did you ever try to not identify with your experiences of same-sex attraction?

11. How old were you when you integrated your same-sex attractions into a lesbian, gay, or bisexual identity?

12. Describe the process you went through to get from thinking of yourself as possibly lesbian, gay, or bisexual to identifying yourself as so (i.e., from "maybe" to "I am"):

13. How long would you say you have lived with an integrated or synthesized lesbian, gay, or bisexual identity?

**PLEASE HAND PARTICIPANT PAGE 160
(DEMOGRAPHICS)
AND ASK HIM/HER TO COMPLETE IT.**

DIRECTIONS:
If the participant answered "(B)" to the question on page 153, please ask the following questions:

1. Looking back, please comment on whether or not you felt different from others for gender-related reasons, for example, because of your choice of play activities as a child (e.g., trucks vs. dolls, house vs. cops and robbers)?

2. Were you ever confused about your same-sex attraction when most of your peers may not have been experiencing same-sex attraction? Tell me what that was like.

3. What do you think contributed to your questioning your sexual identity?

4. What role, if any, did the following factors play in your attributing your same-sex attractions to a lesbian, gay, or bisexual identity? (Check all that apply):
   ❏ Family (parents, siblings)
   ❏ Peer group
   ❏ Religious community
   ❏ Religious literature (Bible, Torah, Koran, etc.)
   ❏ Gay/Lesbian/Bisexual literature
   Comments:

5. Did you ever attribute your experiences of same-sex attraction to anything other than a possible lesbian, gay, or bisexual identity? If so, please explain:

6. Was there a time when you identified yourself publicly as heterosexual?

7. Was there a time when you identified yourself privately (just to yourself) as heterosexual?

8. Before fully dis-identifying with your experiences of same-sex attractions, what . . .
   (a) hindered this process?

   (b) encouraged this process?

9. Did you ever re-appraise your decision to dis-identify with your experiences of same-sex attraction following your initial dis-identification of same-sex attractions?

10. Did you ever try to identify with your experiences of same-sex attraction—to take on a lesbian, gay, or bisexual identity?

11. How old were you when you chose not to identify with your experiences of same-sex attraction?

12. Describe the process you went through to get from thinking of yourself as possibly not lesbian, gay, or bisexual to identifying yourself as not (i.e., from "maybe I am not" to "I am not"):

13. How long would you say you have lived with an integrated or synthesized identity that is not lesbian, gay, or bisexual?

PLEASE HAND PARTICIPANT PAGE 160 (DEMOGRAPHICS) AND ASK HIM/HER TO COMPLETE IT.

Questionnaire

Instructions:

We are interested in your responses to the following questions. Please note that you do not have to complete this questionnaire. Although there are no known risks or discomforts associated with this study, please understand that it is impossible to anticipate all possible risks associated with participation in this study and that the consequences of participation in this research are unpredictable.

The following paragraph is required by Regent University for all research: Regent University, its agents, trustees, administrators, faculty and staff from all claims, damages or suits, not limited to those based upon or related to any adverse effect upon you which may arise during or develop in the future as a result of my participation in this research. Please understand that this release of liability is binding upon you, your heirs, executors, administrators, personal representatives, and anyone else who might make a claim through or under you.

Demographics

Race: o **White**   o **Latino**   o **Black**   o **Asian**   o **Other:** _____

Sex: o **Male**   o **Female**

Age: _____

Sexual orientation:
- o **Heterosexual**
- o **Bisexual**
- o **Homosexual**

Please circle the number that best represents your current sexual orientation:

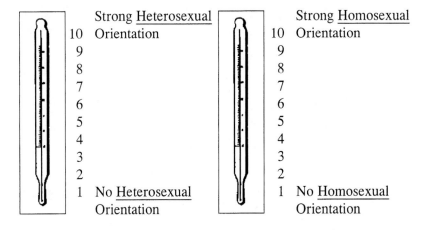

Please circle the number that best represents your current sexual attraction:

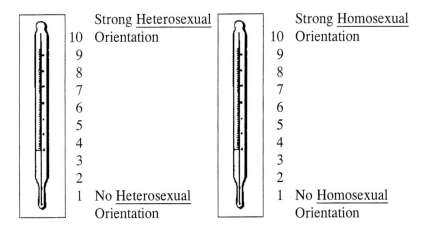

What was your religious affiliation growing up (before age 15)?
o Buddhism   o Hinduism   o Islam   o Judaism
o Protestant Christianity (denomination: _____)
o Catholic Christianity
o None   o Other: _____

What is your religious affiliation now?

o Buddhism   o Hinduism   o Islam   o Judaism

o Protestant Christianity (denomination: _____)

o Catholic Christianity

o None   o Other: _____

How religious do you consider yourself to be?

1	2	3	4	5	6	7	8	9	10
Not religious		Mildly religious		Moderately religious		Somewhat religious		Very religious	

How spiritual do you consider yourself to be?

1	2	3	4	5	6	7	8	9	10
Not spiritual		Mildly spiritual		Moderately spiritual		Somewhat spiritual		Very spiritual	

1.   How has your religion <u>helped</u> your ability to cope with SSA?

_____

_____

_____

_____

2.   How has your religion <u>hurt</u> your ability to cope with SSA?

_____

_____

_____

_____

3. What <u>specific</u> suggestions do your have for how the local church, synagogue, or other religious community could formally support Persons who experience SSA?

_____

_____

_____

_____

Religious Commitment Inventory

PART IV **DIRECTIONS: After each of the following 10 statements, circle one of the numbers that best describes how true the statement is true of you.**

1. My religious beliefs lie behind my whole approach to life.

Not at all true of me	Somewhat true of me	Moderately true of me	Mostly true of me	Totally true of me
1	2	3	4	5

2. I spend time trying to grow in understanding of my faith.

Not at all true of me	Somewhat true of me	Moderately true of me	Mostly true of me	Totally true of me
1	2	3	4	5

3. It is important to me to spend periods of time in private religious thought and reflection.

Not at all true of me	Somewhat true of me	Moderately true of me	Mostly true of me	Totally true of me
1	2	3	4	5

4. Religious beliefs influence all my dealings in life.

Not at all true of me	Somewhat true of me	Moderately true of me	Mostly true of me	Totally true of me
1	2	3	4	5

5. Religion is especially important to me because it answers many questions about the meaning of life.

Not at all true of me	Somewhat true of me	Moderately true of me	Mostly true of me	Totally true of me
1	2	3	4	5

6. I often read books and magazines about my faith.

Not at all true of me	Somewhat true of me	Moderately true of me	Mostly true of me	Totally true of me
1	2	3	4	5

7. I enjoy working in the activities of my religious organization.

Not at all true of me	Somewhat true of me	Moderately true of me	Mostly true of me	Totally true of me
1	2	3	4	5

8. I enjoy spending time with others of my religious affiliation

Not at all true of me	Somewhat true of me	Moderately true of me	Mostly true of me	Totally true of me
1	2	3	4	5

9. I keep well informed about my local religious group and have some influence on its decisions.

Not at all true of me	Somewhat true of me	Moderately true of me	Mostly true of me	Totally true of me
1	2	3	4	5

10. I make financial contributions to my religious organization.

Not at all true of me	Somewhat true of me	Moderately true of me	Mostly true of me	Totally true of me
1	2	3	4	5

Thank you for completing this interview and questionnaire!

Appendix B

Questionnaire for LGB-Identified Participants

1. Thank you for taking time to answer this questionnaire. Before we begin, we would like to give you the opportunity to "tell your story." That is, can you tell us about your experiences of same-sex attraction and how you came to identify yourself as gay or lesbian?

_____

_____

_____

_____

2. Some people cope with their experiences of same-sex attraction by connecting it to the "big picture" about who God is or what life is about. How do you connect your present sexual identity to this "big picture?"

_____

_____

_____

_____

3. As a child, did you feel different from others for gender-related reasons (for example, choice of play activity, style of dress)?

❑ No
❑ Yes,
      reasons included: ❑ My play activities as a child.
                               ❑ My playmates as a child.
                               ❑ Things other people said to me about my behavior or way of relating.
                               ❑ Feelings I had about myself.
                               ❑ Feelings I had about others.
                               ❑ Feelings I had about my parents.
                               ❑ Other reason (please explain):

                                  _____

                                  _____

4. Did you ever experience tension or confusion about your feelings of same-sex attraction when most of your peers (childhood/ adolescent) may not have had the same attractions?

❑ No
❑ Yes,
    I tried to make meaning of the tension/confusion by saying to myself,
                                ❑ "I am a different sex" (for example, "I was the opposite sex.")
                                ❑ "Something is wrong with me"
                                ❑ "I am damaged"
                                ❑ These attractions signify who I really am.
                                ❑ This is just a passing phase.
                                ❑ It really is okay for me to feel this way.
                                ❑ I am looking for a replacement parent.
                                ❑ Other reason (please explain):

                                  _____

                                  _____

5. How old were you when you first noticed that you had feelings of same-sex attraction?

        _____ years old.

6. Think about when you first became aware that there might be a con-
    nection between homosexuality and yourself. What happened to cause
    that awareness?

    ❑ I felt like I was different from other people. (that is, I thought I
       was a different kind of person).
    ❑ I noticed that my feelings about members of the same-sex were
       different from other people.
    ❑ Others told me that I was different from other people because of
       the way I acted.
    ❑ Other people made fun of me because I was different.
    ❑ Other (please explain):

    _____

What feelings did you have about this awareness? Please check all that
apply:

❑ Confused   ❑ Scared   ❑ Angry   ❑ Sad   ❑ Lonely   ❑ Happy
❑ Other feelings (please list):

_____

7. Did you initially think that same-sex attraction meant you were gay
    or lesbian?

    ❑ No, I thought it meant (please check all that apply):

                        ❑ I wanted someone to love me.
                        ❑ I really wanted to be friends with that
                           person I was attracted to.
                        ❑ I was feeling lonely.
                        ❑ I was "sick" or mentally ill.
                        ❑ Other reason (please explain):

                        _____
                        _____

    ❑ Yes, I thought I was gay or lesbian because of my same-sex
       attraction. I started questioning my sexual identity because (of)
       (please check all that apply):

❑ Other people's reactions to me (for example, comments from peers or family members).

❑ Fantasies about same-sex individuals.

❑ I had same-sex attractions.

❑ Other people's behaviors towards me that suggested same-sex attraction (that is, people of the same-sex coming onto me).

❑ Sexual abuse.

❑ No matter what I tried, I couldn't change the feelings of same-sex attraction.

❑ Dating people of the opposite sex did not make me feel the way it made other people feel (for example, excited, aroused).

❑ Other reason (please explain):

_____

_____

8. When you first began to think that you really were gay or lesbian, what did you do about it?

❑ Sought out other gay or lesbian individuals.

❑ Sought out counseling to sort through the confusion.

❑ Sought out counseling to change my sexual orientation.

❑ Sought out information in gay or lesbian literature.

❑ Sought out objective information on homosexuality.

❑ Sought out same-sex sexual experiences.

❑ Sought out sexual experiences with members of the opposite sex.

❑ Avoided any thoughts or feelings related to feelings of same-sex attraction.

❑ Avoided any appearances of homosexuality.

❑ Prayed for God to cure me.

❑ Talked to my parents.

❑ Denied these attractions because of feelings of shame.

❑ Other reason (please explain):

_____

9. Before you initially identified as gay or lesbian, did anything (for example, gay or lesbian literature, religious literature) or anyone (for example, family or friends) affect how you thought about your feelings of same-sex attraction by pointing out that it was suggestive of a gay or lesbian identity?

_____

_____

_____

_____

10. Prior to initially identifying as gay or lesbian, did you have reasons for thinking, "I'm really not gay or lesbian"? Please check all that apply:

❑ No, I never did have reasons for thinking I wasn't gay or lesbian.

❑ Yes, some
   reasons were: ❑ "I am married."
   ❑ "I am dating someone of the opposite sex"
   ❑ "I don't have stereotypical gay male or lesbian behaviors or mannerisms."
   ❑ "It's just sex, I was experimenting."
   ❑ "I like members of the opposite sex also."
   ❑ "My family won't approve/love me."
   ❑ "It doesn't fit my plan for the future."
   ❑ "People will hate or reject me."
   ❑ Other reason (please explain):
   _____

11. Before you identified with your feelings of same-sex attraction, did you ever go through a period of time where you thought or felt your experiences were due to something other than a possible gay or lesbian identity? Please check all that apply:

❑ No, I always thought that same sex attraction meant I was gay or lesbian.

❑ Yes, I thought . . . ❑ same-sex attraction was the result of deficits in parental relationships.
❑ same-sex attraction signaled emotional
dependency.
❑ same-sex attraction was related to sexual
abuse.
❑ same-sex attraction was indicative of personal weakness.
❑ Other reason (please explain):

_____

12. Before you achieved your current sexual identity synthesis, was there
a time when you identified yourself *privately* (just to yourself) as
heterosexual?

❑ Yes
❑ No

13. Before you achieved your current sexual identity synthesis, was there
a time when you identified yourself *publicly* as heterosexual?

❑ Yes
❑ No

14. Before you achieved your current sexual identity synthesis, was there
a time when you identified yourself *privately* (just to yourself) as gay
or lesbian?

❑ Yes
❑ No

15. Before you achieved your current sexual identity synthesis, was there
a time when you identified yourself *publicly* as gay or lesbian?

❑ Yes
❑ No

16. Before you first achieved your current sexual identity synthesis, how old were you when you identified yourself *privately* (just to yourself) as gay or lesbian?

    _____ years old.
    ❏ I never identified myself privately as gay or lesbian.

17. Before you first achieved your current sexual identity synthesis, how old were you when you identified yourself *publicly* as gay or lesbian?

    _____years old.
    ❏ I never identified myself publicly as gay or lesbian.

18. Before you fully identified and achieved your current sexual identity synthesis with your experiences of same-sex attractions (that is, declaring that your feelings of same-sex attraction mean that you are gay or lesbian), what *hindered* this process? Please check all that apply:
    ❏ The effects of sexual abuse (for example, intimacy issues).
    ❏ The stigma of homosexuality in society.
    ❏ Negative family relationships.
    ❏ Negative peer relationships.
    ❏ Fear of hurting my family.
    ❏ Denial of my feelings of same-sex attraction.
    ❏ Emotional cost (loss of support).
    ❏ Spiritual cost (for example, fear that the church/religion, God would reject me).
    ❏ Other reasons (please explain):

    _____

19. Before you fully identified with your experiences of same-sex attractions (that is, declaring that your feelings of same-sex attraction mean that you are gay or lesbian), what *encouraged* this process?
    ❏ Having contacts in the gay or lesbian community.
    ❏ An intimate and personal relationship with someone of the same sex.

❑   Having a family member who is gay or lesbian.
❑   Feelings of same-sex attraction.
❑   Experiences or sexual behavior with someone of the same-sex.
❑   Psychological crisis (that is, "If I don't, I'm going to die")
❑   Other reasons (please explain):

_____

20. When you began re-thinking a gay or lesbian sexual identity (that is, thinking that you might be gay or lesbian), how did your religious/ spiritual worldview help or guide you through this process? Please check all that apply:

❑   It helped me to cope by seeking out a supportive spiritual community.
❑   It helped me to seek the Lord in prayer and worship.
❑   I realized—in prayer or revelation—that Biblical truth was not contrary to a gay or lesbian sexual identity, so that gave me strength to persevere through this process.
❑   It did not help or enter the picture.
❑   I was not accepted in church.
❑   Other reasons (please explain):

_____

21. Please tell us about some of the thoughts you had at this time when you were re-thinking that you might be gay or lesbian before accepting a gay or lesbian identity. (That is, "Am I or am I not gay or lesbian?")

_____

_____

_____

_____

22. What feelings did you have when you accepted the identity of "gay" or "lesbian"? Please check all that apply:

❑ Joy   ❑ Sadness   ❑ Anger   ❑ Peace   ❑ Relief
❑ Fear   ❑ Self-acceptance   ❑ Encouragement
❑ Other feelings (please list):

---

23. What feelings did you have when you first encountered others who had also identified with their experiences of same-sex attraction? Please check all that apply:

❑ Encouragement   ❑ Joy   ❑ Relief   ❑ Peace   ❑ Self-acceptance
❑ Other feelings (please list):

---

24. After you initially decided that you identified yourself as gay or lesbian did you ever *re-think* this decision?

    ❑ No, after I initially decided, I
      never rethought that decision.
    ❑ Yes, I rethought the decision to identify because of
            ❑ my feelings of guilt and shame.
            ❑ the emotional cost identifying.
            ❑ the financial cost.
            ❑ a lack of support from family.
            ❑ a lack of support from friends.
            ❑ a lack of support from a local church.
            ❑ Other reasons (please explain):

If "Yes" you did *re-think* your decision to identify as being gay or lesbian what helped you to adopt a gay identity?

    ❑ More fulfilling intimate relationships with members of the same sex.
    ❑ My relationship with God.
    ❑ The emotional cost of not being in the lifestyle.
    ❑ Financial cost.
    ❑ Lack of support from family.

❑ Lack of support from friends.
❑ Lack of support from a local church.
❑ Other reasons (please explain):

_____

25. Did you ever *try to not identify* with your experiences of same-sex attraction?

❑ No
❑ Yes, I tried not
    to identify   ❑ because it was not easy.
                       ❑ because I didn't want to be in the lifestyle.
                       ❑ because I didn't want to live as an out-
                          cast.
                       ❑ Other reason (please explain):

                          _____

26. How old were you when you first attained your current sexual identity synthesis?

    _____ years old.

27. Which factors helped you to get from thinking of yourself as possibly gay or lesbian to identifying yourself as certainly (that is, from "maybe I am" to "I am")? (Please check all that apply).

❑ I always knew.
❑ My first sexual relationship with a member of the same-sex.
❑ My first emotional relationship with a member of the same-sex.
❑ It felt natural to me.
❑ I accepted my experiences of same-sex attraction as who I really
   am (that is, I accepted myself).
❑ The gay, lesbian and bisexual community supported me.
❑ I always knew that I was gay or lesbian.
❑ Other reasons (please explain):

_____

28. How did your religious or spiritual worldview help you to deal with the stress and tension of the process of identifying as gay or lesbian?

   ❏ I prayed for strength and comfort.
   ❏ Worship helped to alleviate the stress, anxiety or tension.
   ❏ My faith gave me a reason to press through this time of identification.
   ❏ The words of the Lord helped me to persevere.
   ❏ It didn't support me at all.
   ❏ Other reasons (please explain):

   _____

29. How did your religious or spiritual worldview help you to accept and synthesize your current sexual identity?

   ❏ My faith is based on truth and denying my gay or lesbian identity would be contrary to that truth.
   ❏ My faith gave me strength to persevere.
   ❏ My faith has been no help at all.
   ❏ Other reasons (please explain):

   _____

30. Taken all together, how would you say things are these days—would you say that you are very happy, pretty happy, or not too happy?

   ❏ Very happy   ❏ Pretty happy   ❏ Not too happy

   What are some factors that contribute to this rating?

   _____
   _____

Religious Practices and Beliefs

Now we would like to ask you some questions about your religious practices and beliefs. Please circle the answer that you feel is representative of you.

1 = Not at all true of me   4 = Mostly true of me
2 = Somewhat true of me   5 = Totally true of me
3 = Moderately true of me

1. My religious beliefs lie behind my whole approach to life.
   1   2   3   4   5

2. I spend time trying to grow in understanding of my faith.
   1   2   3   4   5

3. It is important to me to spend periods of time in private religious thought and reflection.
   1   2   3   4   5

4. Religious beliefs influence all my dealings in life.
   1   2   3   4   5

5. Religion is especially important to me because it answers many questions about the meaning of life.
   1   2   3   4   5

6. I often read books and magazines about my faith.
   1   2   3   4   5

7. I enjoy working in the activities of my religious organization.
   1   2   3   4   5

8. I enjoy spending time with others of my religious affiliation.
   1   2   3   4   5

9. I keep well informed about my local religious group and have some influence on its decisions.
   1   2   3   4   5

10. I make financial contributions to my religious organization.
   1   2   3   4   5

1 = strongly disagree 3 = moderately agree
2 = moderately disagree 4 = strongly agree

1. My faith involves all of my life.
   1   2   3   4

2. One should seek God's guidance when making every important decision.
   1   2   3   4

3. In my life I experience the presence of the Divine.
   1   2   3   4

4. My faith sometimes restricts my actions.
   1   2   3   4

5. Nothing is as important to me as serving God as best I know how.
   1   2   3   4

6. I try hard to carry my religion over into all my other dealings in life.
   1   2   3   4

7. My religious beliefs are what really lie behind my whole approach to life.
   1   2   3   4

8. It doesn't matter so much what I believe so long as I lead a moral life.
   1   2   3   4

9. Although I am a religious person, I refuse to let religious considerations influence my everyday affairs.
   1   2   3   4

10. Although I believe in my religion, I feel there are many more important things in life.
    1   2   3   4

Appendix B

Demographics

Race: o **White** o **Latino** o **Black** o **Asian** o **Other:** _____

Sex: o **Male** o **Female**

Age: _____

Sexual orientation:
    o **Heterosexual**
    o **Bisexual**
    o **Homosexual**

Please circle the number that best represents your current sexual orientation:

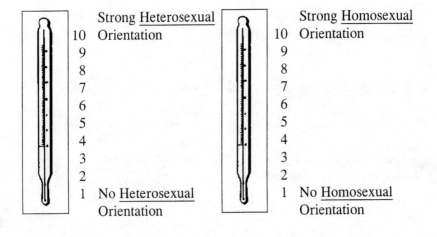

10	Strong <u>Heterosexual</u> Orientation	
9		
8		
7		
6		
5		
4		
3		
2		
1	No <u>Heterosexual</u> Orientation	

10	Strong <u>Homosexual</u> Orientation
9	
8	
7	
6	
5	
4	
3	
2	
1	No <u>Homosexual</u> Orientation

Please circle the number that best represents your current sexual attraction:

10	Strong <u>Heterosexual</u> Orientation	
9		
8		
7		
6		
5		
4		
3		
2		
1	No <u>Heterosexual</u> Orientation	

	Strong <u>Homosexual</u> Orientation
10	
9	
8	
7	
6	
5	
4	
3	
2	
1	No <u>Homosexual</u> Orientation

What was your religious affiliation growing up (before age 15)?
o Buddhism   o Hinduism   o Islam   o Judaism
o Protestant Christianity (denomination: _____)
o Catholic Christianity
o None   o Other: _____

What is your religious affiliation now?

o Buddhism   o Hinduism   o Islam   o Judaism

o Protestant Christianity (denomination: _____)

o Catholic Christianity

o None   o Other: _____

How religious do you consider yourself to be?

1	2	3	4	5	6	7	8	9	10
Not religious		Mildly religious		Moderately religious		Somewhat religious		Very religious	

How spiritual do you consider yourself to be?

1	2	3	4	5	6	7	8	9	10
Not spiritual		Mildly spiritual		Moderately spiritual		Somewhat spiritual		Very spiritual	

31. How has your religion/faith <u>helped</u> your ability to cope with same-sex attractions?

_____

_____

_____

_____

32. How has your religion/faith <u>hurt</u> your ability to cope with same-sex attractions?

_____

_____

_____

_____

33. What <u>specific</u> suggestions do your have for how the local church, synagogue, or other religious community could formally support persons who experience same-sex attractions?

_____

_____

_____

_____

Thank you for completing this interview and questionnaire!

Appendix C

Questionnaire for Dis-Identified Participants

1. Thank you for taking time to answer this questionnaire. Before we begin, we would like to give you the opportunity to "tell your story." That is, can you tell us about your experiences of same-sex attraction and how you came to identify yourself as gay or lesbian?

_____

_____

_____

_____

2. Some people cope with their experiences of same-sex attraction by connecting it to the "big picture" about who God is or what life is about. How do you connect your present sexual identity to this "big picture?"

_____

_____

_____

_____

3. As a child, did you feel different from others for gender-related reasons (for example, choice of play activity, style of dress)?

    ❏ No
    ❏ Yes,

    reasons included: ❏ My play activities as a child.
                         ❏ My playmates as a child.
                         ❏ Things other people said to me about my behavior or way of relating.
                         ❏ Feelings I had about myself.
                         ❏ Feelings I had about others.
                         ❏ Feelings I had about my parents.
                         ❏ Other reason (please explain):

    _____

    _____

4. Did you ever experience tension or confusion about your feelings of same-sex attraction when most of your peers (childhood/ adolescent) may not have had the same attractions? Please check all that apply:

    ❏ No
    ❏ Yes,

    I tried to make meaning of the tension/confusion by saying to myself,

                    ❏ "I am a different sex" (for example, "I was the opposite sex.")
                    ❏ "Something is wrong with me"
                    ❏ "I am damaged"
                    ❏ These attractions signify who I really am.
                    ❏ This is just a passing phase.
                    ❏ It really is okay for me to feel this way.
                    ❏ I am looking for a replacement parent.
                    ❏ Other reason (please explain):

    _____

    _____

5. How old were you when you first noticed that you had feelings of same-sex attraction?

    _____ years old.

6. Think about when you first became aware that there might be a connection between homosexuality and yourself. What happened to cause that awareness?

    ❑ I felt like I was different from other people. (that is, I thought I was a different kind of person).

    ❑ I noticed that my feelings about members of the same-sex were different from other people.

    ❑ Others told me that I was different from other people because of the way I acted.

    ❑ Other people made fun of me because I was different.

    ❑ Other (please explain):

    _____

What feelings did you have about this awareness? Please check all that apply:

❑ Confused ❑ Scared ❑ Angry ❑ Sad ❑ Lonely ❑ Happy
❑ Other feelings (please list):

_____

7. Did you initially think that same-sex attraction meant you were gay or lesbian?

    ❑ No. Although I experienced same-sex attraction, I didn't think it meant I was gay or lesbian. I thought it meant (please check all that apply):

        ❑ I wanted someone to love me.
        ❑ I really wanted to be friends with that person I was attracted to.
        ❑ I was feeling lonely.
        ❑ I was "sick" or mentally ill.
        ❑ Other reason (please explain):

        _____

        _____

    ❑ Yes, I thought I was gay or lesbian because of my same-sex attraction. I started questioning my sexual identity because (of) (please check all that apply):

❑ Other people's reactions to me (for example, comments from peers or family members).

❑ Fantasies about same-sex individuals.

❑ I had same-sex attractions.

❑ Other people's behaviors towards me that suggested same-sex attraction (that is, people of the same-sex coming onto me).

❑ Sexual abuse.

❑ No matter what I tried, I couldn't change the feelings of same-sex attraction.

❑ Dating people of the opposite sex did not make me feel the way it made other people feel (for example, excited, aroused).

❑ Other reason (please explain):

_____

_____

[If you experienced same-sex attraction but *never* identified as gay or lesbian, answer only those questions that are <u>underlined</u> or have <u>underlined parts</u>.]

8. When you first began to think that you really were gay or lesbian, what did you do about it? Please check all that apply.

❑ Sought out other gay or lesbian individuals.

❑ Sought out counseling to sort through the confusion.

❑ Sought out counseling to change my sexual orientation.

❑ Sought out information in gay or lesbian literature.

❑ Sought out objective information on homosexuality.

❑ Sought out same-sex sexual experiences.

❑ Sought out sexual experiences with members of the opposite sex.

❑ Avoided any thoughts or feelings related to feelings of same-sex attraction.

❑ Avoided any appearances of homosexuality.

❑ Prayed for God to cure me.

❑ Talked to my parents.

❑ Denied these attractions because of feelings of shame.
❑ Other reason (please explain):

_____

When you first began to consider the meaning of experiences of same-sex attraction, what did you do about it? Please check all that apply:

❑ Sought out other individuals who struggled with same-sex attraction.
❑ Sought out counseling to sort through the confusion.
❑ Sought out counseling to change the feelings of same-sex attraction.
❑ Sought out information in gay or lesbian literature.
❑ Sought out objective information on homosexuality.
❑ Sought out same-sex sexual experiences.
❑ Sought out sexual experiences with members of the opposite sex.
❑ Avoided any thoughts or feelings related to feelings of same-sex attraction.
❑ Avoided any appearances of homosexuality.
❑ Prayed for God to cure me.
❑ Denied these attractions because of feelings of shame.
Other reason (please explain):

_____

9. Before you initially identified as gay or lesbian, did anything (for example, gay or lesbian literature, religious literature) or anyone (for example, family or friends) affect how you thought about your feelings of same-sex attraction by pointing out that it was suggestive of a gay or lesbian identity? [Even if you did not identify as gay or lesbian, was there anything or anyone that affected how you thought about your feelings of same-sex attraction by pointing out that it was suggestive of a gay or lesbian identity?]

_____

_____

_____

_____

10. Prior to initially identifying as gay or lesbian, did you have reasons for thinking, "I'm really not gay or lesbian"? Please check all that apply:

   ❑ No, I never did have reasons for thinking I wasn't gay or lesbian.

   ❑ Yes, some
     reasons were: ❑ "I am married."
                        ❑ "I am dating someone of the opposite sex"
                        ❑ "I don't have stereotypical gay male or lesbian behaviors or mannerisms."
                        ❑ "It's just sex, I was experimenting."
                        ❑ "I like members of the opposite sex also."
                        ❑ "My family won't approve/love me."
                        ❑ "It doesn't fit my plan for the future."
                        ❑ "People will hate or reject me."
                        ❑ Other reason (please explain):

                        _____

11. Before you disidentified with your feelings of same-sex attraction, did you ever go through a period of time where you thought or felt your experiences were due to something other than a possible gay or lesbian identity? [Please answer this question if you experienced same-sex attraction but did not identify as gay or lesbian]. Please check all that apply:

   ❑ No, I always thought that same sex attraction meant I was gay or lesbian.

   ❑ Yes, I thought . . . ❑ same-sex attraction was the result of deficits in parental relationships.
                          ❑ same-sex attraction signaled emotional dependency.
                          ❑ same-sex attraction was related to sexual abuse.
                          ❑ same-sex attraction was indicative of personal weakness.
                          ❑ Other reason (please explain):

                          _____

12. Before you achieved your current sexual identity synthesis, was there a time when you identified yourself *privately* (just to yourself) as heterosexual? [Please answer this question if you experienced same-sex attraction but did not identify as gay or lesbian]

    ❑ Yes
    ❑ No

13. Before you achieved your current sexual identity synthesis, was there a time when you identified yourself *publicly* as heterosexual? [Please answer this question if you experienced same-sex attraction but did not identify as gay or lesbian]

    ❑ Yes
    ❑ No

14. Before you achieved your current sexual identity synthesis, was there a time when you identified yourself *privately* (just to yourself) as gay or lesbian?

    ❑ Yes
    ❑ No

15. Before you achieved your current sexual identity synthesis, was there a time when you identified yourself *publicly* as gay or lesbian?

    ❑ Yes
    ❑ No

16. Before you first achieved your current sexual identity synthesis, how old were you when you identified yourself *privately* (just to yourself) as gay or lesbian?

    _____ years old.

17. Before you first achieved your current sexual identity synthesis, how old were you when you identified yourself *publicly* as gay or lesbian?

    _____years old.

18. Before you fully dis-identified with your experiences of same-sex attraction and achieved your current sexual identity synthesis (that is, declaring that in spite of your feelings of same-sex attraction, you are not identifying as gay or lesbian), what *hindered* this process? [This question is for all respondents] Please check all that apply:

    ❑ My emotional needs were met in a homosexual relationship.
    ❑ Being in the lifestyle met my desire/lust.
    ❑ I felt the lifestyle fit my sense of being/personhood perfectly.
    ❑ Emotional cost (loss of support).
    ❑ I didn't know anyone who "dis-identified."
    ❑ Feelings of ambivalence.
       Other reasons (please explain):

    _____

19. Before fully dis-identifying with your experiences of same-sex attractions (that is, declaring that in spite of your feelings of same-sex attraction, you are not identifying as gay or lesbian), what *encouraged* this process? [This question is for all respondents] Please check all that apply:

    ❑ God's intervention (for example, conviction)
    ❑ Being in the lifestyle was unfulfilling or painful.
    ❑ Programs such as Living Waters or other curriculum from an Exodus group supported me in leaving the lifestyle.
    ❑ People in my life encouraged me to leave the lifestyle (for example, mentors, accountability partner)
    ❑ Conviction of the Holy Spirit.
       Other reasons (please explain):

    _____

20. When you began <u>re-thinking the meaning of your experiences of same-sex attraction</u>, or a gay or lesbian sexual identity (that is, thinking that you might not be gay or lesbian), how did your religious/spiritual worldview help or guide you through this process? Please check all that apply:

    ❑ It helped me to cope by seeking out a supportive spiritual community.
    ❑ It helped me to seek the Lord in prayer and worship.
    ❑ I realized that my religion and a gay or lesbian identity were in contradiction.
    ❑ It did not help me.
    Other reasons (please explain):

    _____

21. Please tell us about some of the thoughts you had at this time when you were re-thinking that you might not be gay or lesbian. <u>Or, if you experienced same-sex attraction, but never identified as gay or lesbian, did you ever re-think that decision to not identify? That is, did you ever consider identifying with those feelings of same-sex attraction?</u>

    _____

    _____

    _____

    _____

22. What feelings did you have when you initially rejected the identity of "gay" or "lesbian"? Please check all that apply:

    ❑ Joy   ❑ Sadness   ❑ Anger   ❑ Peace   ❑ Relief
    ❑ Fear   ❑ Self-acceptance   ❑ Encouragement
    ❑ Other feelings (please list):

    _____

What feelings do you have *now* about rejecting a gay or lesbian identity?

❑ Joy ❑ Sadness ❑ Anger ❑ Peace ❑ Relief
❑ Fear ❑ Self-acceptance ❑ Encouragement
❑ Other feelings (please list):

---

23. What feelings did you have when you first encountered others who had also dis-identified with their experiences of same-sex attraction? [This question is for all respondents] Please check all that apply:

❑ Encouragement ❑ Joy ❑ Relief ❑ Peace ❑ Self-acceptance
❑ Other feelings (please list):

---

24. After you initially rejected the label "gay" or "lesbian" did you ever re-think this decision? [This question is for all respondents] Please check all that apply:

❑ No
❑ Yes—some reasons include
      ❑ the emotional cost of dis-identifying.
      ❑ the financial cost.
      ❑ a lack of support from family.
      ❑ a lack of support from friends.
      ❑ a lack of support from a local church.
      ❑ Other reason (please explain):

If "Yes" what kept you from re-assuming a gay identity? Please check all that apply:

❑ Accountability (for example, prayer partner).
❑ My relationship with God.
❑ Emotional cost of participating in the lifestyle.
❑ Financial cost.
❑ Lack of support from family.
❑ Lack of support from friends.

❑ Lack of support from a local church.
❑ Other reasons (please explain):

_____

25. Did you ever actively *try to identify* with your experiences of same-sex attraction (that is, consider your experiences of same-sex attraction to mean that you were gay or lesbian)? [This question is for all respondents] Please check all that apply:

❑ No
❑ Yes, I identified as gay or lesbian because
        ❑ I didn't think I had a choice.
        ❑ it was easier to—
           emotionally, relationally, etc.
        ❑ Other reasons (please explain):

        _____

26. How old were you when you first attained your current sexual identity synthesis? This item is for all respondents]

_____ years old.

Please tell us about any situations that lead to the resurgence of same-sex attraction.

_____

_____

_____

_____

How do you understand these experiences? What are some triggers of same-sex attraction?

_____

_____

_____

_____

27. Which factors helped you to get from thinking of yourself as possibly not gay or lesbian to identifying yourself as not (that is, from "maybe I am not" to "I am not")? [Or, if you never identified as gay or lesbian, what factors helped you through the process of not identifying with your experiences of same-sex attraction?] Please check all that apply:

    ❑ Gender identity affirmation (that is, people helped me to develop my masculinity or femininity).
    ❑ God met my emotional needs.
    ❑ I was obedient to God's calling on my life.
    ❑ I was dissatisfied with the relationship.
    ❑ I learned not to trust my feelings.
    ❑ I am still in process; I am still being transformed.
    ❑ I accepted myself and realized that my experiences of same-sex attraction are not who I really am.
    ❑ Other reasons (please explain):

    _____

28. How did your religious or spiritual worldview help you to deal with the stress and tension of the process of dis-identifying with your experiences of same-sex attraction, or as gay or lesbian?

    ❑ I prayed for strength and comfort.
    ❑ Worship helped to alleviate the stress, anxiety or tension.
    ❑ My faith gave me a reason to persevere in this time of identification.
    ❑ God's word (for example, the Bible) helped me to persevere.
    ❑ Other reasons (please explain):

    _____

29. How did your religious or spiritual worldview help you to accept and synthesize your current sexual identity? This question is for all respondents]

    ❑ My faith is based on truth and accepting a gay or lesbian identity would be contrary to that truth.
    ❑ My faith gave me strength to persevere.

❑ I prayed for a new sexual identity.
❑ Other reasons (please explain):

_____

30. Taken all together, how would you say things are these days—would
you say that you are very happy, pretty happy, or not too happy?

❑ Very happy   ❑ Pretty happy   ❑ Not too happy

What are some factors that contribute to this rating?

_____

_____

Religious Practices and Beliefs

Now we would like to ask you some questions about your religious practices and beliefs. Please circle the answer that you feel is representative of you.

1 = Not at all true of me   4 = Mostly true of me
2 = Somewhat true of me   5 = Totally true of me
3 = Moderately true of me

1. My religious beliefs lie behind my whole approach to life.
    1   2   3   4   5

2. I spend time trying to grow in understanding of my faith.
    1   2   3   4   5

3. It is important to me to spend periods of time in private religious thought and reflection.
    1   2   3   4   5

4. Religious beliefs influence all my dealings in life.
    1   2   3   4   5

5. Religion is especially important to me because it answers many questions about the meaning of life.
    1   2   3   4   5

6. I often read books and magazines about my faith.
    1   2   3   4   5

7. I enjoy working in the activities of my religious organization.
    1   2   3   4   5

8. I enjoy spending time with others of my religious affiliation.
    1   2   3   4   5

9. I keep well informed about my local religious group and have some influence on its decisions.
    1   2   3   4   5

10. I make financial contributions to my religious organization.
    1   2   3   4   5

1 = strongly disagree   3 = moderately agree
2 = moderately disagree   4 = strongly agree

1. My faith involves all of my life.
    1   2   3   4

2. One should seek God's guidance when making every important decision.
    1   2   3   4

3. In my life I experience the presence of the Divine.
    1   2   3   4

4. My faith sometimes restricts my actions.
    1   2   3   4

5. Nothing is as important to me as serving God as best I know how.
    1   2   3   4

6. I try hard to carry my religion over into all my other dealings in life.
    1   2   3   4

7. My religious beliefs are what really lie behind my whole approach to life.
    1   2   3   4

8. It doesn't matter so much what I believe so long as I lead a moral life.
    1   2   3   4

9. Although I am a religious person, I refuse to let religious considerations influence my everyday affairs.
    1   2   3   4

10. Although I believe in my religion, I feel there are many more important things in life.
    1   2   3   4

Demographics

Race: o **White**   o **Latino**   o **Black**   o **Asian**   o **Other:** _____

Sex: o **Male**   o **Female**

Age: _____

Sexual orientation:
    o **Heterosexual**
    o **Bisexual**
    o **Homosexual**

Please circle the number that best represents your current sexual orientation:

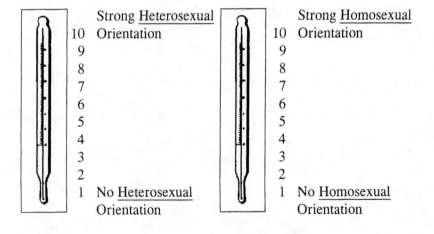

	Strong <u>Heterosexual</u>		Strong <u>Homosexual</u>
10	Orientation	10	Orientation
9		9	
8		8	
7		7	
6		6	
5		5	
4		4	
3		3	
2		2	
1	No <u>Heterosexual</u> Orientation	1	No <u>Homosexual</u> Orientation

Please circle the number that best represents your current sexual attraction:

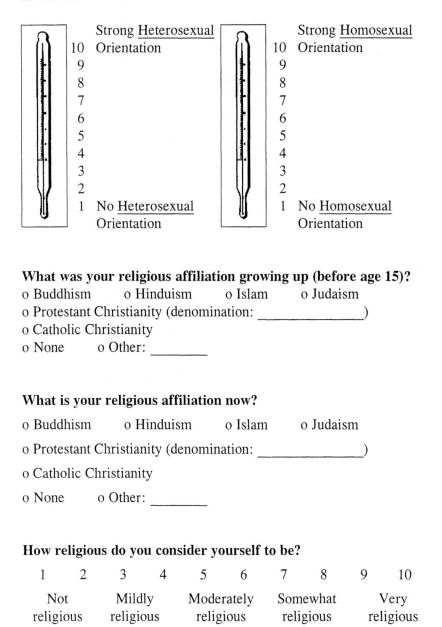

Strong Heterosexual
10 Orientation
9
8
7
6
5
4
3
2
1 No Heterosexual
   Orientation

Strong Homosexual
10 Orientation
9
8
7
6
5
4
3
2
1 No Homosexual
   Orientation

What was your religious affiliation growing up (before age 15)?
o Buddhism　　o Hinduism　　o Islam　　o Judaism
o Protestant Christianity (denomination: ＿＿＿＿＿＿＿＿)
o Catholic Christianity
o None　　o Other: ＿＿＿＿＿

What is your religious affiliation now?

o Buddhism　　　o Hinduism　　　o Islam　　　o Judaism

o Protestant Christianity (denomination: ＿＿＿＿＿＿＿＿)

o Catholic Christianity

o None　　o Other: ＿＿＿＿＿

How religious do you consider yourself to be?

1	2	3	4	5	6	7	8	9	10
Not religious		Mildly religious		Moderately religious		Somewhat religious		Very religious	

How spiritual do you consider yourself to be?

1	2	3	4	5	6	7	8	9	10
Not spiritual		Mildly spiritual		Moderately spiritual		Somewhat spiritual		Very spiritual	

31. How has your religion/faith <u>helped</u> your ability to cope with same-sex attractions?

_____

_____

_____

_____

32. How has your religion/faith <u>hurt</u> your ability to cope with same-sex attractions?

_____

_____

_____

_____

33. What <u>specific</u> suggestions do your have for how the local church, synagogue, or other religious community could formally support persons who experience same-sex attractions?

_____

_____

_____

_____

Thank you for completing this interview and questionnaire!

Endnotes

Chapter One: Models of Sexual Identity Development

1. Vivian C. Cass, "Homosexual identity: A concept in need of definition," *Journal of Homosexuality*, 1984, Vol. 9, No. 2-3, p. 110.

2. Edward Stein, *The Mismeasure of Desire: The Science, Theory, and Ethics of Sexual Orientation* (New York: Oxford, 1999), p. 97.

3. Mark A. Yarhouse & Stanton L. Jones, "A Critique of Materialist Assumptions in Research on Homosexuality," *Christian Scholar's Review*, 1997, Vol. 26, No. 4, p. 482.

4. Edward Stein, *Mismeasure of Desire*, p. 97.

5. Stanton L. Jones & Mark A. Yarhouse, *Homosexuality: The Use of Scientific Research in the Church's Moral Debate* (Downers Grove, IL: InterVarsity Press, 2000), p. 85.

6. J. Michael Bailey, M. P. Dunne & N. G. Martin, "Genetic and environmental influences on sexual orientation and its correlates in an Australian twin sample," *Journal of Personality and Social Psychology,* 2000, Vol. 78, pp. 28-38; cf., J. Michael Bailey & Richard Pillard, "A genetic study of male sexual orientation," *Archives of General Psychiatry,* 1991, Vol. 48, pp. 1089-1096; J. Michael Bailey & Kenneth J. Zucker, "Childhood sex-typed behavior and sexual orientation: A conceptual analysis and quantitative review," *Developmental Psychology,* 1995, Vol. 31, pp. 43-55.

7. Dean Hamer, Stella Hu, V. Magnuson, N. Hu & A. Pattatuci, "A linkage between DNA markers on the X chromosome and male sexual orientation, *Science,* 1993, Vol. 261, pp. 321-327; Stella Hu, A. Pattatuci, C. Patterson, L. Li, D. Fulker, S. Cherny, L. Kruglyak, & Dean Hamer, "Linkage between sexual orientation and chromosome Xq28 in males but not in females," *Nature Genetics,* 1995, Vol. 11, pp. 248-256.

8. G. Rice, C. Anderson, N. Risch, & G. Ebers, "Male homosexuality: Absence of linkage to microsatellite markers at Xq28," *Science,* 1999, Vol. 284 (April 23), pp. 665-667.

9. Simon LeVay, "A difference in the hypothalamic structure between heterosexual and homosexual men," *Science, 253* (1992), pp. 1034-1037.

10. D. Swaab & M. Hofman, "An enlarged suprachiasmatic nucleus in homosexual men," *Brain Research, 537* (1990), pp. 141-148.

11. Irving Bieber, H. J. Dain, P. R. Dince, M. G. Drellich, H. G. Grand, R. H. Gundlach, M. W. Kremer, A. H. Rifkin, C. B. Wilber & Toby B. Bieber, *Homosexuality: A psychoanalytic study* (New York: Basic Books, 1962); Richard B. Evans, "Childhood parental relationships of homosexual men," *Journal of Consulting and Clinical Psychology,* 1969, Vol. 33, pp. 129-135.

12. Andrew P. Bell, M. S. Weinberg, & S. K. Hammersmith, *Sexual preference: Its development in men and women* (Bloomington, IN: Indiana University Press, 1981); Martin Siegelman, "Parental backgrounds of homosexual and heterosexual women: A cross-national replication," *Archives of Sexual Behavior,* 1981, Vol. 10, pp. 371-378.

13. Edward O. Laumann, John H. Gagnon, R. T. Michael, S. Michael, *The Social organization of sexuality: Sexual practices in the United States* (Chicago, IL: The University of Chicago Press, 1994). According to the authors, likelihood of identifying as homosexual tripled among those who reported childhood sexual abuse. Of those who had been sexually abused as children, 7.4% of men and 3.1% of women reported a homosexual orientation; of those not sexually abused, 2.0% of men and 0.8% of women reported a homosexual orientation.

14. Robert A. J. Gagnon, *The Bible and Homosexual Practice* (Nashville, TN: Abingdon Press, 2001).

15. Laumann et al., *The Social organization of sexuality.*

16. *Ibid.,* p. 293.

17. *Ibid.,* p. 294.

18. *Ibid.,* p. 294.

19. *Ibid.,* p. 296.

20. *Ibid.,* p. 297.

21. *Ibid.,* p. 300.

22. *Ibid.,* p. 301.

23. Douglas C. Haldeman, "Therapeutic responses to sexual orientation: Psychology's evolution," In B. Greene & G.L. Croom (Eds.) *Education, research, and practice in lesbian, gay, bisexual, and transgendered psychology: A resource manual,* 2000, (Thousand Oaks, CA: Sage), pp. 255.

24. J. H. McConnell, "Lesbian and gay male identities as paradigms," in S.L. Archer (Ed). *Interventions for adolescent identity development, 1994* (Thousand Oaks, CA: Sage Focus Edition, vol. 169), p. 117.

25. For an interesting discussion of this, see A. Lee Beckstead, "Cure versus choices: Agendas in sexual reorientation therapies," *Journal of Gay and Lesbian Psychotherapy, 2001,* Vol. 5, No. 3/4, pp. 87-115.

26. It should be noted that identity theories and traditional formulations of developmental psychology tend to be more "essentialist," and some theorists take a more "constructivist" approach to sexual identity; see, for example,

Celia Kitzinger, "Social constructionism: Implications for lesbian and gay psychology. In Anthony R. D'Augelli and Charlotte J. Patterson (Eds.), *Lesbian, gay and bisexual identities of ther lifespan: Psychological perspectives* (pp. 136-161), New York: Oxford University Press.

27. Vivian C. Cass, "Homosexual identity."

28. Vivian C. Cass, V.C. (1991) The implications of homosexual identity formation for the Kinsey model and scale of sexual preference. In D. P.McWhirter, S.A. Sanders, & J.M. Reinisch (Eds.), *Homosexuality/heterosexuality: Concepts of sexual orientation. The Kinsey Institute series, Vol. 2. (pp. 239-266).*

29. Eli Coleman, "Developmental stages of the coming out process," *Journal of Homosexuality, 1981, Vol. 7, No.* 2-3, pp. 31-43.

30. *Ibid.*, p. 33.

31. *Ibid.*, p. 33.

32. *Ibid.*, p. 35.

33. *Ibid.*, p. 35.

34. *Ibid.*, p. 36.

35. Richard R. Troiden, "The formation of homosexual identities," *Journal of Homosexuality,* 1989, Vol. 17, No. 1/2, pp. 43-73.

36. J. Grace, "Afirming gay and lesbian adulthood. In N. J. Woodman (Ed.), *Lesbian and gay lifestyles: A guide for counseling and education,* 1992 (New York: Irvington), pp. 33-47.

37. See Kathleen Y. Ritter, & Anthony I. Terndrup, *Handbook of Affirmative Psychotherapy with Lesbians and Gay Men,* 2002 (New York, NY: The Guilford Press).

38. For example, Vivian C. Cass, "Homosexual identity"; Richard R. Troiden, "The formation".

39. S. Cox, & C. Gallois, "Gay and lesbian identity development: A social identity perspective," *Journal of Homosexuality,* 1996, Vol. 30, No. 4, pp. 1-30.

40. *Ibid.*, p. 11.

41. *Ibid.*, p. 16.

42. J. L. Horowitz, & M. D. Newcomb, "A multidimensional approach to homosexual identity," *Journal of Homosexuality, 2001, Vol. 42,* No. 2, pp. 1-17.

43. *Ibid.*, p. 3.

44. *Ibid.*, p. 11.

45. *Ibid.*, p. 12.

46. *Ibid.*, p. 13.

47. *Ibid.*, p. 16.

48. Early theorists discussed "homosexual" identity development; however, this phrase has recently been dropped in favor of gay identity development, as a broad, over-arching label that is meant to refer to lesbian, gay male, and

bisexual identity development. The reasoning is that the word "homosexual" has been associated with psychopathology and mental illness because of its past inclusion in the *Diagnostic and Statistical Manual of Mental Disorders*. We use the word "homosexual" when theorists, such as Cass, used that word; otherwise, we try to follow the more current use of "gay," though there are times when the word "gay" refers more to the sociocultural movement known as the "gay movement", a movement about identity as much as orientation, and we find it helpful at times to distinguish between same-sex attraction, homosexual orientation, and gay identity.

49. G. J. McDonald, "Individual differences in the coming out process for gay men: Implications for theoretical models," *Journal of Homosexuality*, 1982, Vol. 8, No. 1, pp. 47-60.

50. Richard R. Troiden, "Becoming homosexual: A model of gay identity acquisition," *Psychiatry*, 1979, Vol. 42, No. 4, pp. 362-373; Richard R. Troiden & E. Goode, "Variables related to the acquisition of a gay identity," *Journal of Homosexuality, 1980*, Vol. 5, No. 4, pp. 383-392.

51. H. L. Minton, & G. A. McDonald, "Homosexual identity formation as a developmental process," *Journal of Homosexuality*, 1984, Vol. 9, No. 2-3, pp. 91-104.

52. J. Habermas, *Communication and the evolution of society* (Boston, MA: Beacon Press, 1979).

53. Minton & McDonald, "Homosexual identity formation," p. 92.

54. *Ibid.*, p. 96.

55. *Ibid.*, p. 97.

56. *Ibid.*, p. 99.

57. Troiden, "Becoming homosexual."

58. *Ibid.*, p. 367.

59. Laura S. Brown, "Lesbian identities: Concepts and issues," In Anthony R. D'Augelli, & Charlotte J. Patterson (Eds.), *Lesbian, gay and bisexual identities over the lifespan* (New York, NY: Oxford University Press, 1995), p. 7.

60. C. Kitzinger, & S. Wilkinson, "Transitions from heterosexuality to lesbianism: The discursive production of lesbian identities," [Electronic version] *Developmental Psychology*, 1995, Vol. 31, No. 1, 95-104.

61. *Ibid.*, "Going On: Posttransition" section, ¶ 1.

62. J. Sophie, "A critical examination of stage theories of lesbian identity development," *Journal of Homosexuality, 1986*, Vol. 12, No. 2, pp. 39-51.

63. *Ibid.*, p. 49.

64. *Ibid.*, p. 50.

65. *Ibid.*, p. 39.

66. B. E. Chapman & J. C. Brannock, "Proposed model of lesbian identity development: An empirical examination," *Journal of Homosexuality, 1987*, Vol. 14, No. 3/4, pp. 69-80.

67. S. R. McCarn & R. E. Fassinger, "Revisioning sexual minority identity formation: A new model of lesbian identity and its implications for counseling and research," *The Counseling Psychologist,* 1996, Vol. 24, No. 3, pp. 508-534.

68. *Ibid.,* p. 518.

69. *Ibid.,* p. 520.

70. *Ibid.,* p. 520.

71. *Ibid.,* p. 520.

72. Sophie, "A critical examination," p. 49.

Chapter Two: Emerging Trends in Sexual Identity Theory

1. M. J. Eliason, "Identity formation for lesbian, bisexual and gay persons: Beyond a "minoritizing" view. *Journal of Homosexuality, 1996, Vol. 30,* No. 3, pp. 31-55.

2. *Ibid.,* p. 826.

3. J. E. Marcia, "The relational roots of identity," in J. Kroger (Ed.) *Discussions on ego identity* (Hillsdale, NJ: Lawrence Erlbaum Associates, 1993), pp. 101-120.

4. Eliason, "Identity formation," p. 827.

5. *Ibid.,* p. 827.

6. *Ibid.,* p. 828.

7. *Ibid.,* p. 829.

8. Roger L. Worthington, H. B. Savoy, F. R. Dillon and E. R. Vernaglia, "Heterosexual identity development: A multidimensional model of individual and social identity," *The Counseling Psychologist,* 2002, Vol. 10, No. 4, pp. 496-531.

9. *Ibid.,* p. 510.

10. *Ibid.,* p. 510.

11. *Ibid.,* p. 512.

12. *Ibid.,* p. 512.

13. *Ibid.,* p. 515.

14. *Ibid.,* p. 516.

15. *Ibid.,* p. 515.

16. *Ibid.,* p. 516.

17. *Ibid.,* p. 516.

18. J. J. Mohr, "Heterosexual identity and the heterosexual therapist: An identity perspective on sexual orientation dynamics in psychotherapy," *The Counseling Psychologist,* 2002, Vol. 10, No. 4, pp. 532-566.

19. *Ibid.,* p. 536.

20. *Ibid.,* p. 536.

21. *Ibid.,* p. 538.

22. *Ibid.*, p. 539.

23. *Ibid.*, p. 540.

24. *Ibid.*, p. 542.

25. *Ibid.*, p. 542.

26. *Ibid.*, p. 545.

27. *Ibid.*, p. 550.

28. Ron C. Fox, "Bisexual identities," in Anthony R. D'Augelli and Charlotte J. Patterson (Eds.), *Lesbian, gay, and bisexual identities over the lifespan: Psychological perspectives* (New York and Oxford: Oxford University Press, 1995), pp. 48-86; Ron C. Fox "Bisexuality: An examination of theory and research," in R. P. Cabaj, and T. S. Stein (Eds.) *Textbook of homosexuality and mental health* (Washington, DC: American Psychiatric Press, Inc., 1996), pp. 147-171.

29. Exceptions include the models we discuss below, as well as the research by Fritz Klein, who studied sexual orientation with respect to sexual attraction, fantasy, and behavior, as well as self-identification and social and emotional preferences. See Fritz Klein, B. Sepekoff, and T. J. Wolf, "Sexual orientation: A multi-variable dynamic process," *Journal of Homosexuality, 11* (1), (1985), pp. 35-49.

30. Fox, "Bisexual identities," p. 53.

31. M. S. Weinberg, C. J. Williams, and D. W. Pryor, "Becoming bisexual," in *Dual attraction: Understanding bisexuality* (New York, NY: Oxford University Press, 1994), pp. 26-38.

32. *Ibid.*, p. 26.

33. *Ibid.*, pp. 34-35.

34. See Ron C. Fox, "Bisexual identities."

35. *Ibid.*, p. 65.

36. E. M. Dube, and Ritch C. Savin-Williams, "Sexual identity development among ethnic-minority male youths," *Developmental Psychology, 1999, Vol. 35*, No. 6, pp. 1389-1398; Ritch C. Savin-Williams, "Ethnic- and sexual-minority youth," in R. C. Savin-Williams and K. M. Cohen (Eds.), *The lives of lesbians, gays, and bisexuals: Children to adults* (Fort Worth, TX: Harcourt Brace, 1996), pp. 393-415.

37. Savin-Williams, "Ethnic- and sexual-minority youth."

38. Kathleen Y. Ritter, and Anthony I. Terndrup, *Handbook of Affirmative Psychotherapy with Lesbians and Gay Men,* 2002 (New York, NY: The Guilford Press).

39. As conceptualized by D. R. Atkinson, G. Morten and D. W. Sue, (Eds.) *Counseling American minorities: A cross-cultural perspective* (Madison, WI: Brown and Benchmark, 1993).

40. Ritter and Terndrup, *Handbook*, p. 192

41. *Ibid.* p. 193.

42. *Ibid.* p. 194.

43. *Ibid.* p. 194.

44. E. S. Morales, "Counseling Latino gays and Latina lesbians," in S. H. Dworkin and F. J. Gutierrez (Eds.), *Counseling gay men and lesbians: Journey to the end of the rainbow* (Alexandria, VA: American Association for Counseling and Development, 1992), pp. 125-139.

45. Ritter and Terndrup, *Handbook.*

46. Morales, "Counseling Latino," as cited in Ritter and Terndrup, *Handbook*, p. 197.

47. Ritter and Terndrup, *Handbook.*

48. For example, see A. Lee Beckstead, "Cure versus choices: Agendas in sexual reorientation therapies," *Journal of Gay and Lesbian Psychotherapy, 2001,* Vol. 5, No. 3/4, pp. 87-115; Mark A. Yarhouse, "Sexual Identity Development: The Influence of Valuative Frameworks on Identity Synthesis," *Psychotherapy*, Vol., 38, No. 3, pp. 331-341.

49. Beckstead, "Cure versus choices," pp. 87-115.

50. S. R. McCarn & R. E. Fassinger, "Revisioning sexual minority identity formation: A new model of lesbian identity and its implications for counseling and research," *The Counseling Psychologist,* 1996, Vol. 24, No. 3, p. 520.

51. Yarhouse, "Sexual Identity Development."

52. *Ibid.*, p. 335.

53. Mark A. Yarhouse, Erica S. N. Tan, and Lisa M. Pawlowski, "Sexual Identity Development and Synthesis Among LGB-Identified and LGB Dis-Identified Persons," manuscript submitted for review.

54. Yarhouse, "Sexual Identity Development," p. 339.

Chapter Three: The Population and Study

1. A person might also seek out specific communities of like-minded others who affirm similar religious/spiritual beliefs and values that are referred to as gay affirming. For example, a person who identifies as Christian may join a Metropolitan Community Church that is explicitly gay-affirming or participate in a local mainline Protestant church that is gay-affirming despite the broader denomination being more traditional in its teaching about the moral status of same-sex behavior.

2. Erin Blades, p. 49. The Gay Gene: What Does It Matter?, *The Peak*, and reprinted in Homosexuality: Opposing Viewpoints. Quotation found on: http://www.angelfire.com/scifi/dreamweaver/quotes/qthomo.html.

3. See Robert L. Spitzer, "Two Hundred Subjects who Claim to Have Changed their Sexual Orientation from Homosexual to Heterosexual," in Philip A. Bialer (Chair), Clinical Issues and Ethical Concerns Regarding Attempts to Change Sexual Orientation: An Update. Paper presented at the annual meeting of the American Psychiatric Association, New Orleans, Louisiana, 9 May 2001;

cf., A. Lee Beckstead, "Cure versus choices: Agendas in sexual reorientation therapies," *Journal of Gay and Lesbian Psychotherapy, 2001,* Vol. 5, No. 3/4, pp. 87-115.

4. Andrew Comisky, *Pursuing sexual wholeness: How Jesus heals the homosexual* (Lake Mary, FL: Creation House, 1989), p. 38.

5. See Beckstead, "Cure versus choices."

6. Michelle Wolkomir, "Wrestling With the Angels of Meaning: The Revisionist Ideological Work of Gay and Ex-gay Christian Men," *Symbolic Interaction,* 2001, Vol 24, No. 4, pp. 407-424; "Emotion Work, Commitment, and the Authentication of the Self: The Case of Gay and Ex-gay Christian Support Groups," *Journal of Contemporary Ethnography,* 2001, June, Vol 30, No. 3, pp 305-334.

7. It should be noted, too, that this is not just a debate between those who are more gay-affirmative and those who conserve the church's historical teaching about the moral status of same-sex behavior. This is a broader debate about hermeneutics and lenses of interpretation.

8. See Robert A. J. Gagnon, *The Bible and Homosexual Practice: Texts and Hermeneutics,* 2001 (Nashville, TN: Abingdon Press).

9. There are a number of other religion-based paraprofessional ministries, such as Homosexuals Anonymous Fellowship Services (Protestant, non-denominational), Courage (Catholic), Jews Offering New Alternatives to Homosexuality (JONAH; Jewish), Evergreen International (Latter Day Saints or Mormon), and a number of independent, religion-based ministries.

10. The phrase "freedom from homosexuality" is common in Exodus circles. It sometimes suggests change of sexual orientation, as we quote. At other times, it seems to imply the discontinuation of same-sex behavior and the dis-affiliation with the gay community.

11. Mark A. Yarhouse, Erica S. N. Tan, & Lisa M. Pawlowski, "Sexual Identity Development and Synthesis Among LGB-Identified and LGB Dis-Identified Persons," manuscript submitted for review. Initial findings from this pilot study were first presented at the Christian Association for Psychological Studies conference: Mark A. Yarhouse, Erica S. N. Tan & Lisa M. Pawlowski, "Sexual Identity Synthesis: A Pilot Study," poster presented at the Christian Association for Psychological Studies International Conference, Arlington Heights, Illinois, April 13, 2002.

12. Vivian C. Cass, "Homosexual identity: A Concept in Need of Definition," *Journal of Homosexuality,* 1984, Vol. 9, No. 2-3, pp. 219-235.

13. S. J. Taylor & R. Bogdan, *Introduction to Qualitative Research Methods (2nd ed.)* (New York: John Wiley, 1984).

14. Worthington, Wade, Hight, Ripley, McCullough, Berry, Schmitt, Berry, Bursley, & O'Connor, 2003. (2003 The Religious Commitment Inventory-10: Development, Refinement, and Validation of a Brief Scale for Research and Counseling. *Journal of Counseling Psychology, 50* (1), 84-96.

15. D. R. Hoge, "A validated intrinsic religious motivation scale," *Journal for the Scientific Study of Religion,* 1972, Vol. 11, pp. 369-376.

Chapter Four: Sexual Identity Dilemma

1. Mark A. Yarhouse, "Sexual Identity Development: The Influence of Valuative Frameworks on Identity Synthesis," *Psychotherapy,* Vol., 38, No. 3, pp. 331-341.

2. Erik Erikson, *Childhood and Society* (New York: W. W. Norton, 1963).

3. See, for example, Vivian C. Cass, "Homosexual Identity: A Concept in Need of Definition," *Journal of Homosexuality,* 1984, Vol. 9, No. 2-3, pp. 219-235.

4. G. Remafedi, M. Resnick, R. Blum & L. Harris, "Demography of Sexual Orientation in Adolescents," *Pediatrics,* 1992, Vol. 89, No. 4, pp. 714-721.

5. See Edward O. Laumann, John H. Gagnon, R. T. Michael, S. Michael, *The Social Organization of Sexuality: Sexual Practices in the United States* (Chicago, IL: The University of Chicago Press, 1994).

6. Cass, "Homosexual Identity."

7. Eli Coleman, "Developmental Stages of the Coming out Process," *Journal of Homosexuality,* 1981, Vol. 7, No. 2-3, pp. 31-43.

8. Richard R. Troiden, "The Formation of Homosexual Identities," *Journal of Homosexuality,* 1989, Vol. 17, No. 1/2, pp. 43-73.

9. Grace, "Afirming Gay and Lesbian Adulthood."

10. H. L. Minton, & G. A. McDonald, "Homosexual Identity Formation as a Developmental Process," *Journal of Homosexuality,* 1984, Vol. 9, No. 2-3, pp. 91-104.

11. J. Sophie, "A Critical Examination of Stage Theories of Lesbian Identity Development," *Journal of Homosexuality,* 1986, Vol. 12, No. 2, pp. 39-51.

12. B. E. Chapman & J. C. Brannock, "Proposed Model of Lesbian Identity Development: An Empirical Examination," *Journal of Homosexuality,* 1987, Vol. 14, No. 3/4, pp. 69-80.

13. Diamond, 1998, p. 1085.

14. *Ibid.,* p. 1085.

15. Michelle Wolkomir, "Wrestling with the Angels of Meaning: The Revisionist Ideological Work of Gay and Ex-gay Christian Men," *Symbolic Interaction,* 2001, Vol 24, No. 4, pp. 407-424; "Emotion Work, Commitment, and the Authentication of the Self: The Case of Gay and Ex-gay Christian Support Groups," *Journal of Contemporary Ethnography,* 2001, June, Vol 30, No. 3, pp 305-334.

16. Cass, "Homosexual Identity."

17. Troiden, "The Formation of Homosexual Identities."

18. Grace, "Affirming gay and lesbian adulthood."
19. Chapman & Brannock, "Proposed Model."
20. S. R. McCarn & R. E. Fassinger, "Revisioning Sexual Minority Identity Formation: A New Model of Lesbian Identity and its Implications for Counseling and Research," *The Counseling Psychologist,* 1996, Vol. 24, No. 3, pp. 508-534.
21. Our understanding of the construct of homophobia is really still in its infancy. Although there are several measures of homophobia, none is without significant limitations, although we anticipate that the construct itself will be understood better over time as more research is conducted in this area.

Chapter 5: Sexual Identity Development

1. Edward Stein, *The Mismeasure of Desire: The Science, Theory and Ethics of Sexual Orientation* (New York: Oxford, 1999), p. 97.
2. As we mentioned in Chapter 1, constructionists claim that sexual orientation is really a linguistic construct developed to describe sexual preferences. The labels heterosexual, homosexual, and bisexual are "social human kinds" (Stein, 1999, p. 97) more likened those we use to describe political preferences, as when we refer to Republicans and Democrats. Laumann et al (1994) suggests that most researchers in the area of human sexuality are actually constructionists who rely on essentialist categories when conducting research.
3. Vivian C. Cass, "Homosexual Identity: A Concept in Need of Definition," *Journal of Homosexuality*, 1984, Vol. 9, No. 2-3, p. 230.
4. For example, Richard R. Troiden, "Becoming Homosexual: A Model of Gay Identity Acquisition," *Psychiatry*, 1979, Vol. 42, No. 4, pp. 362-373; G. J. McDonald, "Individual Differences in the Coming Out Process for Gay Men: Implications for Theoretical Models," *Journal of Homosexuality*, 1982, Vol. 8, No. 1, pp. 47-60.
5. E. M. Dube, & Ritch C. Savin-Williams, "Sexual Identity Development among Ethnic-minority Male Youths," *Developmental Psychology*, 1999, Vol. 35, No. 6, pp. 1389-1398.
6. Diamond, "Development of Sexual Orientation among Adolescent and Young Adult Women," *Developmental Psychology*, 1998, Vol. 34, No. 5, pp. 1085-1095.
7. Interestingly, Cass (1991) acknowledges that it is still possible to foreclose on identification as LGB: "Because human beings are intentional creatures who have the capacity to act on as well as be acted on by their sociocultural context, some individuals will dynamically engage with their environment so as to prevent the acquisition of a lesbian or gay self-understanding. This process is termed 'foreclosure.'" (p. 233). However, the use of the term 'fore-

closure' might be interpreted by some as a derogatory characterization and not a full and sympathetic understanding of an alternative sexual identity synthesis.

8. Cass, "Homosexual Identity."

9. Eli Coleman, "Developmental Stages of the Coming Out Process," *Journal of Homosexuality*, 1981, Vol. 7, No. 2-3, pp. 31-43.

10. For a discussion of a helpful coping and meaning-making model, see Park & Folkman (1997). Crystal L. Park & Susan Folkman, "Meaning in the Context of Stress and Coping," *Review of General Psychology*, 1997, Vol. 1, No. 2, 115-144.

11. See Kathleen Y. Ritter, & Anthony I. Terndrup, *Handbook of Affirmative Psychotherapy with Lesbians and Gay Men*, 2002 (New York, NY: The Guilford Press).

12. As we consider attributions it is important to remember the limitations of retrospective research. It is certainly possible that an individual can "fill in the blanks" of their memory of attributions based on present identity and commitments. With this in mind, we have decided to accept participants' attributions and sense of meaning at face value, while remembering that by asking these questions of both LGB-identified and LGB-dis-identified participants, the limitations of retrospective research apply to both groups.

13. E. M. Dube, & Ritch C. Savin-Williams, "Sexual Identity Development among Ethnic-minority Male Youths," *Developmental Psychology*, 1999, Vol. 35, No. 6, p. 1390.

14. See Robert L. Spitzer, "Two Hundred Subjects who Claim to Have Changed their Sexual Orientation from Homosexual to Heterosexual," in Philip A. Bialer (Chair), Clinical Issues and Ethical Concerns Regarding Attempts to Change Sexual Orientation: An Update. Paper presented at the annual meeting of the American Psychiatric Association, New Orleans, Louisiana, May 9, 2001. Interestingly, Spitzer reported that, on average, it took 2 years for those who reported experiencing a change in their sexual orientation to begin to experience this change, and an average of 5 years to fully realize the change.

15. Kim W. Schaeffer, L. Nottebaum, P. Smith, K. Dech, & J. Krawczyk, "Religiously Motivated Sexual Orientation Change: A Follow-up Study, *Journal of Psychology and Theology*, 1999, Vol. 27, pp. 329-337.

16. The original sample a year earlier consisted of 248 participants of which 208 had given permission to be contacted for a follow-up study, so there may be others who: are still attempting change, unsure whether to continue to pursue it, or are no longer attempting it. See Kim W. Schaeffer Schaeffer, R. A. Hyde, T. Kroencke, B. McCormick, & L. Nottebaum, "Religiously Motivated Sexual Orientation Change," *Journal of Psychology and Christianity*, 2000, Vol. 19, No. 1, pp. 61-70.

Chapter 6: Sexual Identity Synthesis

1. For examples, see G. J. McDonald, "Individual Differences in the Coming out Process for Gay Men: Implications for Theoretical Models," *Journal of Homosexuality*, 1982, Vol. 8, No. 1, pp. 47-60; J. Sophie, "A Critical Examination of Stage Theories of Lesbian Identity Development," *Journal of Homosexuality*, 1986, Vol. 12, No. 2, pp. 39-51.

2. Richard R. Troiden, "Becoming Homosexual: A Model of Gay Identity Acquisition," *Psychiatry*, 1979, Vol. 42, No. 4, pp. 362-373.

3. Eli Coleman, "Developmental Stages of the Coming out Process," *Journal of Homosexuality*, 1981, Vol. 7, No. 2-3, pp. 31-43.

4. Grace, "Affirming Gay and Lesbian Adulthood."

5. McDonald, "Individual Differences."

6. B. E. Chapman & J. C. Brannock, "Proposed Model of Lesbian Identity Development: An Empirical Examination," *Journal of Homosexuality*, 1987, Vol. 14, No. 3/4, pp. 69-80.

7. Sophie, "A Critical Examination."

8. Ariel Shidlo & Michael Schroeder, "Changing Sexual Orientation: A Consumers' Report," *Professional Psychology: Research and Practice*, 2002, Vol. 33, No. 3, pp. 249-259.

9. Interestingly, 26 of the participants in the Shidlo and Schroeder study perceived themselves to be successful in making a "heterosexual shift," and these were further categorized as (1) successful/struggling (n = 12), (2) successful/not struggling (n = 6), and (3) successful shift to heterosexuality (n = 8). Many participants from this convenience sample reported unsuccessful attempts to change their sexual orientation, which may be indicative of the nature of the study itself, which was originally designed to provide empirical support for the claim that reorientation therapies are harmful.

10. *Ibid.*, p. 254.

11. Kim W. Schaeffer, L. Nottebaum, P. Smith, K. Dech, & J. Krawczyk, "Religiously-Motivated Sexual Orientation Change: A Follow-up Study, *Journal of Psychology and Theology*, 1999, Vol. 27, pp. 329-337.

12. The question of whether or not sexual orientation can change through involvement in professional therapy or paraprofessional ministry involvement is not addressed in this study of sexual identity development and synthesis. In fact, several theorists have discussed the value of focusing on the broader construct of sexual identity rather than the narrow question of change of orientation. It may be conjectured that some of the reports of change of sexual orientation are addressing the broader construct of sexual identity. Although it is difficult to say with certainty, it is interesting that "positive outcomes" from involvement in professional intervention ranges considerably from diminished same-sex attraction and fantasies to increased opposite-sex attraction and fantasies. Others have measured simple behavioral changes.

More recent survey research is generally consistent with the extant data, including MacIntosh's survey of 1215 analysts who reported working with homosexual clients, of whom 276 (23%) remarked to have experienced a positive outcome. The survey published by the National Association for Research and Therapy of Homosexuality reports similar shifts following change efforts. The study by Spitzer also suggests that some people may experience change in at least their sense of their sexual identity and their perception of the sexual orientation. Even those who had not changed as they would have liked, still believed therapy to have been worthwhile and valuable, given their values and vision of quality of life. Again, this may point to the experience of sexual identity synthesis. See Houston MacIntosh, "Attitudes and Experiences of Psychoanalysts," *Journal of the American Psychoanalytic Association*, 1994, Vol. 42, No. 4, pp. 1183-1207; Robert L. Spitzer, "Two Hundred Subjects who Claim to Have Changed their Sexual Orientation from Homosexual to Heterosexual," in Philip A. Bialer (Chair), Clinical Issues and Ethical Concerns Regarding Attempts to Change Sexual Orientation: An Update. Paper presented at the annual meeting of the American Psychiatric Association, New Orleans, Louisiana, May 9, 2001; National Association for Research and Treatment of Homosexuality, "A Survey of Sexual Orientation Change," self-published and distributed by NARTH, 1997; available at http://www.narth.com.

13. Spitzer, "Two Hundred Subjects."

14. In several studies those who identify as LGB report higher elevations than heterosexuals on measures of mental health concerns, including major depression, generalized anxiety disorder, conduct disorder, nicotine dependence, substance abuse or dependence, suicide ideation, suicide attempts, and sexually transmitted diseases. Although discussion continues about causes of these elevations, most in the gay community attribute them to a disapproving society. However, a couple of more recent studies from the Netherlands, clearly one of the world's most gay-affirming societies, also report higher elevations. This facet should therefore be studied further. See Susan D. Cochran, Emerging Issues in Research on Lesbians' and Gay Men's Mental Health: Does Sexual Orientation Really Matter? *American Psychologist*, 2001, Vol. 56, No. 11, pp. 931-947.

15. L. J. Nottebaum, Kim W. Schaeffer, J. Rood, & D. Leffler, "Sexual Orientation: A Comparison Study," unpublished manuscript available from Kim W. Schaeffer, PhD, Department of Psychology, Point Loma Nazarene University, 3900 Lomaland Drive, San Diego, CA 92106.

16. Arlene Swidler (ed.), *Homosexuality and World Religions* (Valley Forge, PA: Trinity Press International, 1993).

17. Michelle Wolkomir, "Wrestling with the Angels of Meaning: The Revisionist Ideological Work of Gay and Ex-gay Christian Men," *Symbolic Interaction*, 2001, Vol 24, No. 4, pp. 407-424.

18. We have, for the most part, purposefully avoided the term "lifestyle" because it communicates something held in common by all who identify as lesbian, gay, or bisexual. However, because several participants used this term in this section, we use it here to accurately reflect their language, also as it was used in some of the options, because participants spoke about lifestyle in the original pilot study.

19. E. M. Dube, & Ritch C. Savin-Williams, "Sexual Identity Development among Ethnic-minority Male Youths," *Developmental Psychology,* 1999, Vol. 35, No. 6, pp. 1389-1398.

20. See Kathleen Y. Ritter, & Anthony I. Terndrup, *Handbook of Affirmative Psychotherapy with Lesbians and Gay Men,* 2002 (New York, NY: The Guilford Press).

21. Wolkomir, "Wrestling."

22. *Ibid.,* p. 408.

23. *Ibid.,* p. 411.

24. *Ibid.,* p. 412.

25. *Ibid.,* p. 414.

26. *Ibid.,* p. 416.

27. *Ibid.,* p. 419.

28. Richard Lints, "Imaging and Idolatry: The Sociality of Personhood and the Ironic Reversals of the Canon," paper presented at the colloquium of the Alliance of Confession Evangelicals, Colorado Springs, Colorado, June 2002.

29. Everett L. Worthington, Jr., Nathaniel G. Wade, Terry L. Hight, Jennifer S. Ripley, Michael E. McCullough, Jack W. Berry, Michelle M. Schmitt, James T. Berry, Kevin H. Bursley, & Lynn O'Connor, "The Religious Commitment Inventory—10: Development, refinement, and validation of a brief scale for research and counseling," *Journal of Counseling Psychology*, 003, Vol. 50, No. 1, pp. 84-96.

Chapter 7: Theory, Research and Practice

1. S. R. McCarn & R. E. Fassinger, "Revisioning Sexual Minority Identity Formation: A New Model of Lesbian Identity and its Implications for Counseling and Research," *The Counseling Psychologist*, 1996, Vol. 24, No. 3, p. 520.

2. Margaret Nichols, Therapy with Sexual Minorities. In. Sandra R. Leiblum & Raymond C. Rosen (ed), *Principles and Practice of Sex Therapy (3rd edition),* 2000 (New York, NY: The Guilford Press), p. 352.

3. *Ibid.,* p. 353.

4. Richard R. Troiden, "The Formation of Homosexual Identities," *Journal of Homosexuality*, 1989, Vol. 17, No. 1/2, p. 61.

5. Barash, p. B11.

6. One reviewer offered that what we may actually be discussing here is another identity, perhaps a "socio-religious" identity, which has other dimensions and might be considered independently of one's sexual identity. In other words, if sexual feelings are not the primary way an individual defines their sense of sexual identity, then is the ensuing identity a sexual identity or a different identity altogether (e.g., a "socio-religious" identity). The question then becomes, Can same-sex attraction be integrated into certain religious identities?

7. Roger Smith, "The Next Chapter of the American Story," *Chronicle of Higher Education*, 2003, Vol.,69, No. 44, pp. B10-11.

8. *Ibid.*, p. B10.

9. *Ibid.*, p. B10.

10. Park & Folkman, 1997.

11. Michelle Wolkomir, "Emotion Work, Commitment, and the Authentication of the Self: The Case of Gay and Ex-gay Christian Support Groups," *Journal of Contemporary Ethnography*, 2001, June, Vol 30, No. 3, pp 305-334.

12. J. H. Dalton, M. J. Elias, & A. Wandersman, *Community Psychology: Linking Individuals and Communities* (Belmont, CA: Wadsworth, 2001), p. 164.

13. We did not have the same experience as Wolkomir. Both the UFMCC and Exodus groups seemed equally accessible, although the response rates varied, perhaps suggesting more interest in participation among those involved in Exodus.

14. Wolkomir, "Emotion Work."

15. Lisa M. Diamond, "Development of Sexual Orientation among Adolescent and Young Adult Women," 1998, *Developmental Psychology*, Vol. 34, No. 5, pp. 1085-1095.

16. Mark A. Yarhouse, Lisa M. Pawlowski, & Erica S. N. Tan, "Intact Marriages in Which One Partner Dis-Identifies with Experiences of Same-Sex Attraction," 2003, *American Journal of Family Therapy*, Vol. 31, pp. 369-388.

17. See Schneider, Brown & Glassgold, 2002.

18. Mark A. Yarhouse & Lori A. Burkett, "An Inclusive Response to LGB and Conservative Religious Persons: The Case of Same-Sex Attraction and Behavior," 2002, *Professional Psychology: Research and Practice*, Vol. 33, No. 3, pp. 235-241.

19. For one example tailored to the experiences of conservative Christian clients, see Mark A. Yarhouse and Lori A. Burkett, *Sexual Identity: A Guide to Loving in the Times between the Times*, 2003 (Lanham, MD: University Press of America).

20. American Psychological Association, "Appropriate Therapeutic Responses to Sexual Orientation in the Proceedings of the American Psychologi-

cal Association, Incorporated, for the Legislative Year 1997," *American Psychologist*, 1998, Vol. 53, No. 8, pp. 882-939.

21. Division 44/Committee on Lesbian, Gay, and Bisexual Clients Joint Task Force, "Guidelines for Psychotherapy with Lesbian, Gay, and Bisexual Clients." *American Psychologist*, 2000, Vol. 55, No. 12, pp. 1440-1451.

22. Margaret S. Schneider, Laura S. Brown, & Judith M. Glassgold, "Implementing the Resolution on Appropriate Therapeutic Responses to Sexual Orientation: A Guide for the Perplexed," *Professional Psychology: Research and Practice*, 2002, Vol. 33, No. 3, pp. 265-276.

23. A. Lee Beckstead & Susan L. Morrow, "Mormon Clients: Experiences with Conversion Therapy: The Need for a New Treatment Approach (in press). *The Counseling Psychologist*.

24. Michelle Wolkomir, "Wrestling with the Angels of Meaning: The Revisionist Ideological Work of Gay and Ex-gay Christian Men," *Symbolic Interaction*, 2001, Vol 24, No. 4, pp. 407-424; "Emotion Work, Commitment, and the Authentication of the Self: The Case of Gay and Ex-gay Christian Support Groups," *Journal of Contemporary Ethnography*, 2001, June, Vol 30, No. 3, pp. 305-334.

25. Wolkomir, "Wrestling," p. 415.

26. *Ibid.*, p. 417.

27. Wolkomir, "Emotion Work," p. 331.

28. *Ibid.*, p. 331.

29. Wolkomir, "Wrestling," p. 422.

30. *Ibid.*, p. 422.

Index

About the Authors

Mark A. Yarhouse, Psy.D., is a licensed clinical psychologist and Associate Professor of Psychology at Regent University in Virginia Beach, Virginia. He received his B.A. degree from Calvin College in 1990, M.A. degree in Clinical Psychology (1993), M.A. degree in Theological Studies (1997), and Psy.D. in Clinical Psychology (1998) from Wheaton College.

Dr. Yarhouse is Director of the Institute for the Study of Sexual Identity at Regent University. He serves on the editorial boards of the *Journal of Family Violence*, *The Family Journal*, *Journal of Psychology and Theology*, and *Marriage and Family: A Christian Journal*. He has contributed articles to *Professional Psychology: Research and Practice*, *Psychotherapy*, and the *American Journal of Family Therapy*. Dr. Yarhouse is co-author of *Homosexuality: The Use of Scientific Research in the Church's Moral Debate* (with Stanton L. Jones) and *Sexual Identity: A Guide to Living in the Time Between the Times* (with Lori A. Burkett).

Erica S.N. Tan, Psy.D., is currently a postdoctoral resident at Eden Counseling Center in Virginia Beach, Virginia. She received her B.A. in psychology from the University of Ottawa in 1995, and her M.A. in Clinical Psychology in 2001 from Regent University. She graduated from Regent University with a Psy.D. in Clinical Psychology in 2004. Dr. Tan's research and clinical interests include adolescents and their families around issues of sexuality and sexual identity.